Table of Contents

NJ ASK4 — Language Arts Literacy

Contributing Writers: Diane O. Barone
Cosmo Lorusso

Acknowledgments:

Excerpt from *The Kite Fighters*, by Linda Sue Park. Reprinted with permission from Random House.
From Knights in Days of Old, by Ellen Javernick. Reprinted with permission by Highlights for Children.
Run, Kate Shelley, Run, by Julia Pferdehirt. Reprinted with permission by Readers Digest Inc.
Endangered Species Problem. Reprinted with permission by The National Geographic Society.

ISBN #978-1-56749-623-9

Instructivision, Inc.
16 Chapin Road • P.O. Box 2004 • Pine Brook, NJ 07058
Phone 973-575-9992 • Fax 973-992-9134
www.instructivision.com

To the Student:

This book will help you to become more familiar with the kinds of questions you will be asked on the Language Arts Literacy section of the New Jersey ASK4 test. By doing the exercises in this book you will be well prepared for the test.

This book has multiple-choice questions, open-ended questions, and writing assignments. In some questions you will have a choice of four answers from which you must choose the correct or the best answer. Other questions ask you to write a short paragraph or an essay on a certain topic.

Practice is the key to success. Learn the skills. Look up unfamiliar words in the dictionary. Use and study them until you know them well. This will help you to do well on the test.

The NJ ASK4 Language Arts Literacy test contains both narrative and informational texts. You will be asked to answer questions based on what you have read. These questions will test your knowledge and understanding of a variety of reading texts. In this section of the workbook, we will review and practice some of those reading skills. The first problem or question in each of the Practice Exercises that follow has been answered for you.

Determining the Main Idea

Determining the author's main idea is an important skill you will need to learn. You will also need to learn to tell the difference between a main idea and a supporting detail. A main idea is usually general in nature and sums up in one sentence the point the author is trying to make. The author can use a few or many details to support his or her main idea. In the supporting sentences the author can provide dates, numbers, facts, opinions, or any other statements to reinforce and explain his or her main idea to the reader.

Practice Exercise 1

Directions: Read each selection and choose the sentence that best states the main idea.

1. The food for most plants is made in the leaves. The leaves also give off water. Cactus plants are different because they have no leaves. Instead, the water is stored in the stem of the plant. The cactus' food is also made in the stem. During dry periods in the desert, the cactus plants may be the only source of water for miles around. If it were not for the sharp points on the cactus plants, many thirsty animals would eat them, and cactuses would have died out long ago.

    What is the main idea of this passage?

    ___ A. There is little food or water in the desert.
    ___ B. The cactus is an unusual plant.
    ___ C. The cactus grows in the desert.
    ___ D. All plants need food and water.

    The correct answer is B. The other choices are supporting details.

2. Milton S. Hershey was born in Pennsylvania in 1857. He attended a one-room school house as a child, and stopped going to school after fifth grade. His family was poor, so young Milton went to Lancaster to work for a printer. Milton didn't like being a printer, so he left to work for a candy maker. Hershey was only 20 years old when he started his own candy business in Philadelphia. At first he was not very successful and he worked in various cities. In 1894 Milton returned to Pennsylvania and formed the Hershey Chocolate Company. This company was a huge success, and Milton Hershey became very rich.

Milton S. Hershey (left)

Hershey built a town around his chocolate factory with homes for his employees, parks, a sports arena, a theater, libraries, a trolley system, and an amusement park for their enjoyment. In 1909 Hershey and his wife, Catherine, who had no children of their own, opened the Hershey Industrial School for orphaned boys. After his wife died he gave all his wealth to the school.

Until his death in 1945 Hershey continued to oversee his huge business, the town and the school. Today, the Hershey Chocolate Company is one of the largest and most successful chocolate companies in the world.

The Milton S. Hershey School, located in Hershey, Pennsylvania, the largest residential school in the United States, is still fully supported from the profits from the Hershey Chocolate Company.

What is the main idea of this passage?

___ A. Milton Hershey failed at candy making several times before succeeding with the Hershey Chocolate Company.
___ B. Although he lacked a good education, Milton Hershey created the most successful chocolate company in the world.
___ C. After Milton Hershey became a great success, he devoted much of his time and wealth to helping others.
___ D. Milton Hershey is best known for building the largest school in the United States.

3. "Shoeless" Joe Jackson began playing professional baseball in 1908 with the Philadelphia Athletics, but he played only 10 games with that team. In 1911 he was traded to Cleveland where he had a .408 batting average, a record that still stands today for a player in his rookie season. In 1915 he was traded to the Chicago White Sox where he continued to be one of the best hitters in baseball. In 1919 the White Sox made it to the World Series. During that year Jackson batted .351 during the regular season and an even higher .375 in the World Series. But the White Sox, who were heavily favored to win, lost the championship to the Cincinnati Reds. The following year, Jackson and seven of his teammates were accused of taking money to deliberately lose the World Series and were suspended from playing. In 1921 a Chicago jury found Jackson not guilty. But the Commissioner of Baseball ignored the court's ruling and banned all 8 players from professional baseball for the rest of their lives.

Jackson's record is impressive. He led the American League in triples in 1912, 1916, and 1920. In fact, Jackson ranked 3rd in all-time batting average with .356, which surpasses even that of Ted Williams and Babe Ruth. Yet, Jackson is not eligible for the Baseball Hall of Fame since he was placed on the ineligible list in 1920. Jackson died in 1951 and his estate has now applied to the office of the Commissioner of Major League Baseball to reinstate him. If the Commissioner does reinstate Jackson, then he would be eligible for consideration by the Baseball Hall of Fame Committee on Baseball Veterans, an honor he definitely earned during his short-lived professional career.

What is the main idea of this passage?

___ A. Joe Jackson was accused of accepting money to deliberately lose a World Series championship.
___ B. Joe Jackson was one of the greatest hitters in baseball, and he belongs in the Hall of Fame.
___ C. The Commissioner of Baseball had no right to ban the White Sox from baseball since a jury had found them not guilty.
___ D. Jackson's fine hitting and fielding during the World Series is proof that he was not trying to lose.

4. When ten-year-old Amelia Mary Earhart saw her first plane at a state fair, she was unimpressed. "It was a thing of rusty wire and wood and looked not at all interesting," she said. It wasn't until she attended a stunt-flying exhibition, almost 10 years later, that she became seriously interested in aviation. A pilot gave her a ride that would change her life forever. "By the time I had got two or three hundred feet off the ground," she said, "I knew I had to fly."

In 1932 Amelia Earhart became the first woman to fly across the Atlantic Ocean alone, establishing a new record for the crossing: 13 hours and 30 minutes. For this flight she was awarded honors by both the American and French governments. In 1935 she became the first woman to fly across the Pacific Ocean when she flew from Hawaii to California. In June 1937 she attempted to fly around the world. With her navigator, Frederick J. Noonan, she left from Miami, Florida. Their plane disappeared on July 2, while flying from New Guinea to Howland Island over the Pacific Ocean. Planes and ships of the United States Navy searched for the missing flyers, but they failed to discover any trace of them, and their fate remains a mystery to this day.

What is the main idea of this passage?

___ A. Although not interested in airplanes at first, Amelia Earhart later became a well-known aviator, remembered for her ground-breaking flights.

___ B. No one knows what became of Amelia Earhart and her navigator, Frederick J. Noonan.

___ C. Amelia Earhart was a brave woman who risked her life to pave the way for other female flyers.

___ D. Amelia Earhart's tragic disappearance near New Guinea is still a mystery.

Practice Exercise 2

Directions: Read each pair of sentences below. Decide which one is the main idea and which is the supporting detail. On the blank line, write either "main" or "detail."

1. The Seeing Eye trains guide dogs for the blind.   *main*

   It was founded in 1929 in Morristown, New Jersey.   *detail*

2. Yahoo, Google, and Lycos are examples of popular internet search engines.   _____

   A search engine helps people find information on the Internet.   _____

3. Asbury Park was once a thriving tourist area.   _____

   In 1871 James Bradley bought a 500-acre tract of woodland and began building a resort.   _____

4. People can listen to audio books while driving in their car, while they are exercising, and even while they are working.   _____

   Audio books are a great alternative to the printed word.   _____

5. Monopoly is sold in 80 countries and produced in 26 languages including Croatian.   _____

   Monopoly is the best-selling board game in the world.   _____

6. Radio broadcasts could be just as frightening as modern horror movies. _____

A 1938 radio broadcast of "War of the Worlds" had many people terrified that aliens were landing in New Jersey. _____

7. Kwanzaa was created by Dr. Maulana Karenga, a scholar and activist. _____

Kwanzaa is the fastest-growing holiday in the United States. _____

8. Several famous comedians came from New Jersey. _____

Bud Abbott was born in Asbury Park, Lou Costello was born in Paterson, and Jerry Lewis was born in Newark. _____

9. The top apple-producing states are Washington, New York, Michigan, California, Pennsylvania, and Virginia. _____

Apples are grown in all 50 states. _____

10. The Statue of Liberty is a symbol of freedom and democracy. _____

Located in the New York Harbor, the Statue of Liberty was a gift of friendship from the people of France to the people of the United States. _____

Finding the Meaning of Words in Context

An important reading skill is determining the meaning of an unknown word by looking for clues in the words, phrases and sentences that surround that word.

Practice Exercise 3

Directions: Read each selection below. Based on the context clues, select the best definition of the underlined word.

1. Although best known for the witch hunts that occurred there in 1692, Salem, Massachusetts, is a city rich in maritime history. Located on the Atlantic coast, Salem's success as a seaport made the town rich and filled it with huge mansions. Sea captains made a fortune trading goods with lands as far away as the West Indies, Asia, and Africa.

    What is the best meaning of the word maritime?

    ___ A. relating to money
    ___ B. relating to the sea
    ___ C. relating to witches
    ___ D. relating to large houses

    Answer: The best choice is B. Note that the sentence starts with **although** *which means that the word maritime is not about witches. The next sentence mentions* **seaport***. You would conclude that it has something to do with sea.*

2. The food guide pyramid is an outline of what you should eat each day. It is not meant to be followed as a rigid command, but as a general guide. Different people have different nutritional needs, and the pyramid lets you choose a healthy diet that's right for you.

    What is the best meaning of the word rigid?

    ___ A. strict
    ___ B. spoken
    ___ C. broad
    ___ D. unhealthy

3. An act of <u>spite</u> led to the invention of one of the most popular snack foods of all time. In 1853 a customer at the Moon's Lake House complained that the chef's French fries were "too thick and soggy." This comment made the chef angry, and he wanted to "get even" with the unhappy customer. He sliced the potatoes paper-thin, fried them until they were golden brown and crispy, heavily salted them, and then gave them to the customer. The chef was surprised when the customer actually enjoyed what was to become later the first potato chips.

   What is the best meaning of the word <u>spite</u>?

   ___ A. hunger
   ___ B. creativeness
   ___ C. humor
   ___ D. meanness

4. Computers have become an <u>integral</u> part of our daily lives. Computers run many of our nation's transportation systems, banks, utilities, and communications companies. If all these computers should suddenly stop working, our world would be in serious trouble.

   What is the best meaning of the word <u>integral</u>?

   ___ A. entertaining
   ___ B. important
   ___ C. unnecessary
   ___ D. modern

5. Not everything offered on a Chinese menu is an <u>authentic</u> dish from China. Chop suey, for instance, is purely American. There are many different stories about when and in what part of our country chop suey was invented, but one thing is certain: it did not come from China.

   What is the best meaning of the word <u>authentic</u>?

   ___ A. vegetable
   ___ B. spicy
   ___ C. genuine
   ___ D. tasty

Drawing Conclusions

Another important reading skill is to be able to "read between the lines." That is, you must be able to draw a conclusion based on information given in the passage. Authors do not always come out and say what is on their mind. It is often necessary for a reader to infer the author's meaning.

<u>Practice Exercise 4</u>

Directions: Read each group of sentences below. Draw a conclusion based on the information given in the sentences.

1. Cats are cleaner than dogs. They can be taught to use a litter box, so you won't have to walk them on a leash like you would a dog. Cats won't keep you or your neighbors awake by barking at night.

    What conclusion can you draw from these sentences?

    Answer:

    <u>Cats make better pets than dogs.</u>

2. Some parents want to control what their children read. They have every right to do so. But do they have the right to say what other people's children should read? When parents ask that books be banned from school libraries, they are making important decisions not only for their own children but for all the children in the school. Isn't there a better way for these concerned parents to control what their children read without depriving others of the works by such great authors as Mark Twain, William Shakespeare and Nathaniel Hawthorne?

    What conclusion can you draw from these sentences?

    _____

    _____

3. People have listened to music in many ways over the years. The early vinyl records could be scratched and would "skip" when you played them. If they were exposed to high heat, the vinyl would warp or melt. Eight-track tapes and cassettes could break while being played. They could also become "demagnetized." Compact discs, however, are almost in-destructible.

What conclusion can you draw from these sentences?

_____

_____

4. I can't imagine not having a cell phone. I use it several times a day. I call my mother when I am late coming home. I talk to my friends when I am lonely. I call my grandfather when I feel like it. I know he loves it when I call him. I remind my father to pick me up at my friend's house. I can call from places where nobody can listen to my conversation.

What conclusion can you draw from these sentences?

_____

_____

5. We spend more money on cosmetics than we do on books. We spend more time going to the beauty parlor or to the gym than we do going to the library. Most of us, if we were to win a lottery, would choose to spend our winnings on plastic surgery rather than on getting a better education.

What conclusion can you draw from these sentences?

_____

_____

Learning the Difference Between Fact and Opinion

Authors often include their own personal beliefs, or opinions, in their writing. They don't always identify these beliefs by saying, "in my opinion." It is up to the reader to determine what is fact (a statement that can be proven) and what is opinion (a belief held by a person, but not necessarily a factual statement).

Practice Exercise 5

Directions: Read each statement below. In the space provided, indicate whether the sentence is a fact or an opinion.

1. Paul Robeson, born in Princeton, New Jersey, was an athlete, actor, singer, scholar and author.   *fact*

2. It is better to take a class trip to a museum than to an amusement park.   _____

3. The New York Yankees won more World Series titles than any other team in baseball history.   _____

4. More students at Midvale Elementary School did better in their social studies test than in their math test.   _____

5. Tom Hanks is a great actor.   _____

6. The movie *Titanic* won an Academy Award for Best Picture of the Year.   _____

7. People who download music over the Internet are stealing from the musicians who record that music.   _____

8. New Jersey is one of the thirteen original colonies.   _____

9. When temperatures reach 90 degrees, it is too hot to go to the beach.   _____

10. There are fewer teams in the Women's National Basketball Association (WNBA) than the men's NBA.   _____

Exercise 1

The Kite Fighters

Excerpt from the book by Linda Sue Park

Young-sup watched as his older brother, Kee-sup, ran down the hill with the kite trailing behind him. The kite bumped and skittered along the ground, but if Kee-sup got up enough speed, it sometimes caught a low puff of wind and rose into the air.

Sometimes.
Not very often.
Every tenth try or so.

In the air the kite would hold steady for several moments, then dive without warning. Kee-sup ran in different directions, pulling

5 desperately on the line, but to no avail. The kite always ended up on the ground with its twin "feet" crumpled beneath it, looking, Young-sup thought, both angry and ashamed.

Young-sup watched silently. He did not bother to ask for a turn; Kee-sup would offer when he was ready. It was his kite, after all.

Kee-sup had been given the kite as a birthday present several days before, as part of the New Year celebration. The New Year was everyone's birthday. It didn't matter on which date you were born; you added a year to your age at the New Year holiday.

Young-sup's gift had been a *yut* set. Normally, he would have been delighted to receive the popular board game, with its little carved men. But when they opened their gifts, his first feeling was one of envy.

His brother's kite was wonderful. It had been purchased from Kite Seller Chung, who made the finest kites in the marketplace. Two huge eyes were painted on it, to help it see its way clear into the skies; heavy eyebrows made it look fierce and determined. Young-sup had to swallow hard to hold back his jealous words.

It hadn't helped that Kee-sup had left immediately to fly the kite on his own. Young-sup had begged and pleaded and pestered for days, and today, at last, Kee-sup had invited him to the hillside to fly.

The snow-dusted hill on which the brothers stood stretched down toward the great wall that surrounded Seoul. The road that wound around the base of the hill led to one of the city's nine enormous gates. Beyond the wall Young-sup could see hundreds of rooftops, huddled together and crouched low to the ground, as if bowing to the palace at the center of the city. The grand tiled roofs of the royal palace stood out in graceful curved splendor. No other structure was permitted to rise higher.

Young-sup continued watching in silence as the kite took yet another dive and crashed. At last Kee-sup handed it over. Young-sup felt a river of eagerness surge through him as he took it.

He had decided to try a different technique. Holding the kite at arm's length in one hand and the reel in the other, he threw the kite up into the air.

It came straight down and would have hit him on the head if he hadn't dodged out of the way.

"I tried that before," said Kee-sup. "A hundred times. It never works."

Young-sup picked up the kite. In that brief moment he had felt why it would not fly.

On only his second try he launched the kite from a complete standstill.

Kee-sup's jaw dropped. "Hey! How did you do that?"

Young-sup shrugged, not wanting to display too much pride. "I'll show you," he said. For he knew in his bones that he could do it again.

The kite flew proudly. Young-sup let it play for a few moments, thrilled at the pull on the line in his hands. Bringing in an arm's length of line, he experimented, plying it to and fro. The kite made graceful figure eights, swooping and dipping like a playful fish. Then Young-sup reeled it in, keeping control until the kite floated just overhead. He gave the line a final, gentle tweak, and the kite drifted to the ground.

Young-sup picked it up and began to demonstrate. "First, you let out some line, not too much but enough to give it a little slack." Holding the middle of the kite in one hand with his arm outstretched, he turned his body slightly. "Then you must stand with the strength of the wind at your back, and hold the kite like so. There will come a moment when the wind is just right. That's when you throw the kite into the air and allow it to take up the extra line."

Young-sup waited a few moments. Then, as if obeying his words, the kite leaped and rose to stretch the line taut. It was as if an invisible hand had pulled the kite into the air.

22

He brought it down again and handed Kee-sup the reel. "Now you try."

Kee-sup arranged the line and held the kite as Young-sup had done, then released it and yanked on the reel. The kite crashed to the ground.

"No, no!" cried Young-sup. "The most important thing is to wait for the right moment."

"How do you know when it's right?" Kee-sup sounded cross.

Young-sup hesitated. "It's right when it—when it . . . Can't you tell?"

"Of course not. That's why I'm asking you, pig-brain."

Young-sup tapped his chin lightly with his fist, thinking. Then he scanned the ground around his feet until he found a slim stick. He used it to

 draw in the powdery snow—a crude sun, a few clouds, a tree. "Look," he said. "If you could draw the wind, what would it look like?" He gave the stick to his brother.

"What do you mean? Wind doesn't *look* like anything."

"Just try."

Kee-sup hesitated, then added a few curving lines to the landscape.

"That's right." Young-sup nodded. "That's what I see when I fly a kite."

"You can't *see* wind."

"I know, I know. But you can *feel* it, right? And you can see what it does."

"The way it moves the trees."

"Yes, the trees . . . but it was more than that." Young-sup spoke slowly, trying to find the right words. "I could tell what the wind is like because the kite—" He glanced at his brother, lowered his eyes, and mumbled, "The kite talked to me."

"The kite *talked* to you?"

"Yes," Young-sup answered, more sure of himself now. "The first time, when I tried throwing it into the air, something said to me, 'More—more line' and 'Wait . . . wait for the wind. . . . *Now!*' It must have been the kite. What else could it be?"

Kee-sup frowned for a moment. Then he laughed suddenly and slapped his knee. "The kite must have a *tok-gabi!*"

Tok-gabis were invisible imps who visited every household from time to time. When the rice burned or an ink pot spilled, such incidents were blamed on a *tok-gabi*. They were mischievous spirits but seldom caused real harm. Young-sup joined his brother in laughter at the thought of a little imp clinging to the kite.

"Perhaps you have somehow angered the *tok-gabi*," Young-sup joked.

"Well, one thing is certain," Kee-sup said. "Whatever language kites speak, I haven't learned it yet."

∞

1. Where is the setting of the story?

    __ A. On a rooftop in the city
    __ B. On a hill overlooking the city
    __ C. In the backyard of the children's home
    __ D. On the playground

2. Why was Young-sup not happy with his birthday present?

    __ A. He did not like board games.
    __ B. His brother's present was more expensive.
    __ C. He wanted a kite like his brother.
    __ D. He wanted a better present than his brother.

3. In paragraph 22, the author writes, "Then, as if obeying his words, the kite leaped and rose to stretch the line taut." Using the context clues, find the best synonym for taut.

    __ A. loose
    __ B. tight
    __ C. high
    __ D. crooked

4. What emotion does Kee-sup display when his brother is able to fly the kite?

    __ A. pride
    __ B. joy
    __ C. fear
    __ D. surprise

5. How does Young-sup explain his ability to fly the kite when his brother cannot?

    __ A. He claimed the kite spoke to him.
    __ B. He claimed he could see the wind.
    __ C. He claimed a spirit helped him.
    __ D. He claimed to know more about kites because he was older.

6. In the last paragraph, Kee-sup states, "Whatever language kites speak, I haven't learned it yet." What does he mean by this?

    __ A. that he must learn to speak the language the kite speaks
    __ B. that he no longer wants to keep the kite
    __ C. that he hasn't yet learned how to properly fly a kite
    __ D. that he isn't as smart at his brother

7. What would be another good title for this story?

    __ A. The Angry *Tok-gabi*
    __ B. Young-sup's Brother
    __ C. Kee-sup's New Year's Present
    __ D. What the Wind *Looks* Like

8. This story can best be described as

    __ A. a folk tale.
    __ B. an autobiography.
    __ C. fiction.
    __ D. a mystery.

9. In the story Kee-sup asked his brother how he was able to fly the kite. Young-sup drew a picture of the sun, the clouds and a tree in the snow and told his brother to draw the wind. Why do you think he did this?

_____

_____

_____

_____

_____

_____

_____

_____

_____

_____

_____

_____

_____

10. Complete a story web for the story you have just read.

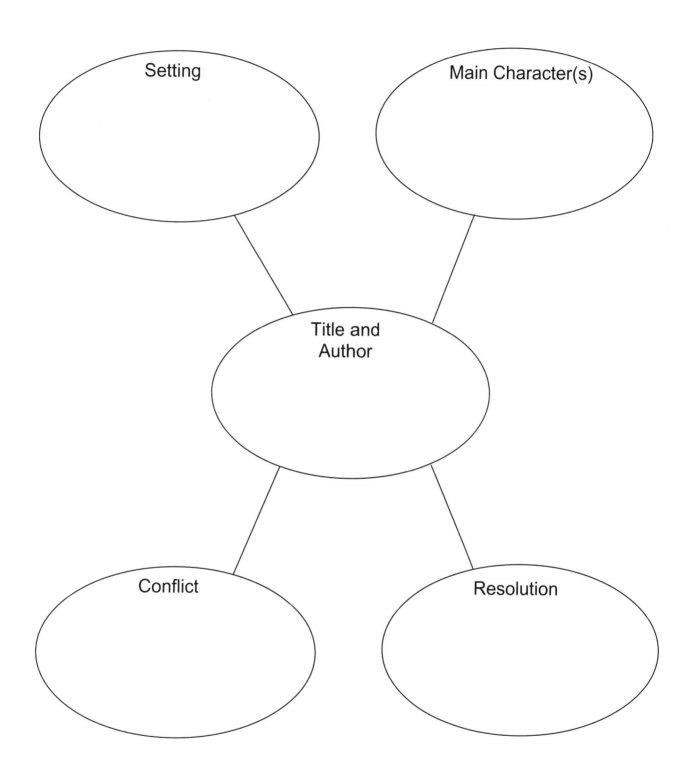

Run, Kate Shelley, Run

by Julia Pferdehirt

Kate Shelley's home stood on a hill above Honey Creek and the railroad line that led to Moingona, Iowa. All her life Kate had heard the rush of water and the whistle of trains. All her life she had watched the Chicago and Northwestern railway cars and heard the hissing, black steam engines clack-clattering over Honey Creek Bridge.

Every train had a number and a whistle. When Kate's father was alive, he had taught her to recognize each train by the sound of its whistle. He'd been a section foreman for the Chicago and North-western until his death three years earlier in a railroad accident. After that, Kate and her mother fed the livestock, planted the garden, and sent the little ones off to school.

3 Kate was fifteen years old in July 1881, when the great storm began. It rained on Friday. By Saturday, market day, the ground was muddy, and still the rain poured down. On Sunday the roads were thick, brown sponges, sucking at boots and wagon wheels. The rain fell day and night. The following Wednesday, the sky paused to catch its breath. The day was oven-hot. Kate rushed to hang laundry to dry before the rain came again. Sure enough, by afternoon she saw more clouds, dark as midnight, rolling toward Honey Creek.

Young Kate Shelley

After nearly a week of rain, the creek was a wild bull, roaring and leaping, crashing against the high bluffs that caged it in on either side. Fence posts, rocks, and entire trees rolled and tumbled down the creek bed, colliding with the pilings of the bridge, causing it to creak and sway. Then the storm broke, and rain poured from the sky. The water rose.

The rising floodwaters began to seep into the barn, and Kate hurried down the hill to rescue the stock. She turned the animals out to higher ground and scrambled to save the baby pigs huddled on a haystack surrounded by water. Then Kate went up to the house and stared anxiously out the windows with her mother and nine-year old sister, Mayme. The younger children were asleep.

It was nearly eleven o'clock when Kate heard Number 11's whistle. Long, short—long, short—screaming into the wind. The rumble of the engine grew louder as it crept along the line from Moingona to Boone, checking for washouts on the track. Suddenly Kate heard a crack like thunder, and another and another. With a sound like cannon fire, the Honey Creek trestle bridge, the engine, and four terrified crewmen crashed into the roaring water twenty feet below.

Kate pulled on her barn coat and a battered straw hat. "I'm going," she said.

Kate's mother gripped her arm. "No, Kate. You could be killed in that storm!"

Kate grabbed Pa's railroad lantern. "If Pa were out there, I'd go," she said. "I have to do it, Ma." With shaking hands, she lit the lantern and ran into the downpour and darkness to Honey Creek.

The water tossed trees and twisted metal like toys. Two men clung to branches surrounded by the wreckage; they were screaming for help. The two other crewmen had been washed away. Kate waved her lantern to say, "Hold on. Just hold on. I'll do something."

Bridge over Honey Creek

Before Kate could think of a way to help the men, a terrible thought struck her. The midnight express was scheduled to come through in less than an hour. The train, its crew, and two hundred passengers were right now, right this minute, headed toward Honey Creek, not realizing that the bridge was out. It had sounded like cannon fire when Number 11 went down. It would sound like an entire war if the midnight express crashed into Honey Creek. Over two hundred people could die. She had to stop that train!

Kate gripped the lantern tighter and stumbled along the rails, following them like a road into the blackness and storm. She ran and fell, slipped and stumbled, toward the Moingona railroad station over a mile away.

Kate's chest burned. She was wet clear through and shaking with cold, but she could not stop. If it were Pa hanging on in Honey Creek or driving the midnight express, she would keep going. I must reach the station in time, she thought.

Between Honey Creek and the Moingona station, the railroad crossed the Des Moines River. The trestle bridge was high above the water and nearly seven hundred feet long. Kate dared not think of the railroad ties, a pace apart, only rain and sky between them and the river below.

The storm shook the Des Moines River bridge until it swayed and trembled. The rain fell even harder. Mud and water made the crossties slick and <u>treacherous</u>. How could anyone cross this bridge—caught between the wind, the rain, and the boiling, angry river? Kate knelt down and crawled forward on her hands and knees. If it were Pa driving the midnight express toward Honey Creek, she would keep crawling. She could crawl for those two hundred people.

The wind blew her lantern out. She crept forward in the dark feeling the railroad ties with her hands, using the cold metal rails as a guide.

Suddenly lightning flashed, and Kate saw a tree hurtling toward the bridge. Its tangled branches and massive trunk rolled and bounced in the current. It would hit the bridge! She remembered the crack of the pilings at Honey Creek and the cannon shot as the trestle collapsed. Kate clung to the crossties and prayed.

At the last second the current flipped the tree so the great trunk and its reaching limbs slipped between the pilings. Even then the branches tried to pull Kate from her perch above the river. She held on tighter and trembled.

"Only a little farther," Kate told herself when her hands finally felt mud and stones instead of empty air between the ties. She was safe across the bridge now; it was a half-mile to the station.

When she saw the station lights, Kate ran like a wild woman. Her wet skirt slapped and caught against her legs. Every breath hurt. She crashed into the station door and fell inside.

"Stop! Stop the train!" she gasped. "The engine—Honey Creek. Stop the train."

"The girl's crazy!" said one of the railroad men.

"Not on your life!" said the station agent. "That's Shelley's girl Kate."

Between gasps for air, Kate told them the Honey Creek bridge had collapsed. "Two men are still alive," she said. "And the midnight express must be stopped."

The station agent telegraphed six miles west to Ogden to be sure the midnight express would not be allowed to continue in the storm. Then the railroad men and Kate boarded a pusher engine and headed toward Honey Creek, blowing the whistle all the way, calling to the two stranded men to hold on a little longer.

At Honey Creek the bluffs had collapsed into the water. Kate led the rescuers to another bridge where they could cross and finally reach the engineer and brakeman. The two men were half-dead with exhaustion.

After that, Kate did not remember the engine puffing away toward the station. She did not remember her mother leading her to bed or piling blankets over her shaking body. She did not remember the gray-and-rose sky of dawn.

The same telegraph that had warned Ogden station to hold the midnight express sent news of Kate's bravery from city to city. Within days, newspapers all over the nation were calling her the "Iowa heroine."

While Kate lay in bed recovering from the terrible night, every train passing the farmhouse blew its whistle in her honor. Then the people of Iowa awarded her a gold medal, and the railroad gave her one hundred dollars and a lifetime railroad pass.

The nation honored Kate, too. However, the honor most dear to her came from the railroad men themselves. As long as she lived in Moingona, Iowa, they recognized brave Kate in their own special way. Whenever she wanted to ride the Chicago and Northwestern, they stopped the train just for her. A station stop was not good enough. They stopped the train right in front of the little farmhouse on Honey Creek.

In 1900 a new bridge was built across the Des Moines River and named for Kate Shelley. And after her death, the Order of Railway Conductors and Brakemen placed a memorial to their Iowa heroine. "Hers is a deed bound for legend . . . a story to be told until the last order fades and the last rail rusts."

Kate Shelley Memorial Park Railroad Museum

1. In paragraph 3 the author writes, "On Sunday the roads were thick, brown sponges, sucking at boots and wagon wheels." This means the streets were

    __ A. very wet and extremely muddy.
    __ B. changed into real sponges.
    __ C. slippery and hilly.
    __ D. filled with slush.

2. In paragraph 15 the author writes, "Mud and water made the crossties slick and treacherous." Using the context clues, what would be the best synonym for treacherous?

    __ A. curious
    __ B. dangerous
    __ C. ruthless
    __ D. wet

3. Why did Kate not stay with the men clinging to the branches?

    __ A. She was not strong enough to pull them out.
    __ B. She did not think they were really in danger.
    __ C. She was cold and wanted to get home.
    __ D. She wanted to stop the midnight express before it crashed into the river.

4. Why is the station agent sure that Kate is telling the truth about the washout?

    __ A. because he knew Kate and trusted her
    __ B. because he knew the bridge was old and in bad shape
    __ C. because he knew that men had fallen into the river
    __ D. because he heard the train whistle

5.	What would be another good title for the story?

	__	A.	Kate Shelley Stops the Train
	__	B.	Kate Shelley Saves the Train
	__	C.	A Storm Destroys Honey Creek
	__	D.	Kate Shelley Saves the Creek

6.	What is the main problem Kate Shelley must solve in the story?

	__	A.	to get home safely during a big storm
	__	B.	to warn a train about danger ahead
	__	C.	to stop a bridge from falling
	__	D.	to save her father's life

7.	Why does Kate Shelley keep mentioning her father and thinking about him, even though he is no longer living?

	__	A.	She feels responsible for her father's death.
	__	B.	She is afraid her mother will be disappointed if she fails.
	__	C.	She has no one else to talk to.
	__	D.	She thinks if he were still alive he would be one of the railroad men whose life was in danger.

8.	In the last paragraph, the phrase "Hers is a deed bound for legend" means

	__	A.	people will be talking about Kate Shelley's heroic action for a long time.
	__	B.	everybody will soon forget what Kate Shelley did.
	__	C.	a movie will be made of the event.
	__	D.	Kate Shelley will be traveling often by train.

9.	This story can best be described as

	__	A.	an autobiography.
	__	B.	science fiction.
	__	C.	fiction.
	__	D.	a biography.

10. The author writes, "Within days newspapers all over the nation were calling her the "Iowa heroine." Do you think Kate Shelley was a heroine? Why or why not?

_____

_____

_____

_____

_____

_____

_____

_____

_____

_____

_____

_____

_____

_____

_____

_____

_____

_____

_____

_____

_____

_____

_____

11. Below is a graphic organizer for the story *Run, Kate Shelley, Run*. Think about the story and recall the important events in the order that they happened. Write the events in the boxes provided. The first one has been done for you.

FIRST:

After nearly a week of rain, the roads in Honey Creek, Iowa, are thick with mud.

NEXT:

NEXT:

LAST:

Exercise 3

The Rich Man's Place
by Horace E. Scudder

The rich man had a splendid place—a house and barns, and a great pleasure park—but it was long since he had seen his place, for he had been traveling abroad.

When people travel abroad, they expect to learn much, and the rich man when he came home had no doubt learned a great many things. He had brought away as much of other countries as he could carry—a little in his head, but a good deal in boxes. When these boxes were unpacked, there were pictures and statues and malachite tables, and at least three cart-loads of curious things, which he arranged about the house, so that when his friends came to see him, they all said it was nearly as well as visiting foreign lands themselves; for when they entered the house, the rich man would remind them where he had been.

"This hat-tree," he would say, as they took off their hats, "is made of wood from the Black Forest," and then they would shut their eyes, and fancy themselves there. "This table on which I keep my clothes-brush," he would continue, "is a malachite table from Russia." And then they would ask him if he saw the Czar. When they entered the parlor, he would take them on a tour about the room, and feed their imagination with a stone from the field of Waterloo, a splinter from John Knox's house, a piece of pottery from Turkey, and a statue from Greece; and, if left to themselves, they were given a book of views, or a stereoscope, or allowed to stand before the étagère, and handle the Swiss toys and Scotch pebbles. Oh, it was precisely the same as going abroad, and so the guests all said.

But it was best when someone came who had traveled, and perhaps with the rich man himself: then the guests would listen as one said to the other, "Do you remember that night on the Riviera?"

And the other would say, "Ah, indeed!" and look knowing. "But the Carnival, ah!" he would rejoin, and turn round to the guests, humming the "Carnival of Venice."

"What a tame country ours is!" the guests would sigh to them-selves. Now the rich man walked over his place when he had unpacked his curiosities. His father and grandfather had lived there before him, and the trees were old and large. It was certainly a noble plantation, but it did

6

not please the rich man. It had had its own way too much, something was wanting—he had been abroad and seen parks—what was it?

"This place needs attention," said he, "and I am determined to improve it." So he bought statues, and placed them about the grounds—plaster statues of young men leaning on hoes, and young girls with aprons full of flowers, and in a basin he set up a statue of Venus rising out of the sea foam. It was an extraordinary thing: a water-pipe ran around the base, and little jets threw out spurts of water which were to cover Venus, and look like a veil.

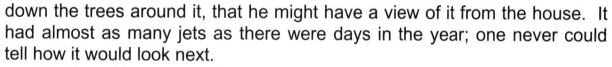

But he did not succeed very well with this, and people found considerable fault with it. He built stone terraces, and ran straight gravel walks so wide that ten could walk abreast, and so long that one could prove the earth was round by watching a man appear at the other end. The cedar trees he had cut after his own taste, and of these he was very proud. The gardener, with a pair of shears, clipped the branches according to certain models. One tree looked like a bear, another like a lion, a third like a giraffe, and in the middle stood one which was like a man.

"Now this is something," said the rich man, admiring it: "still something is lacking. Ah! I know; it is a fountain." So he had a fountain made and cut down the trees around it, that he might have a view of it from the house. It had almost as many jets as there were days in the year; one never could tell how it would look next.

"I believe I have everything after my mind now," said he, "and I will give a festival for all my neighbors. The poor people, too, shall be allowed to come in and stay at a distance. They will make the scene picturesque." He gave out word of the festival, and you may be sure everybody was delighted to come, for his grounds had been kept shut, and it was said that wonderful improvements had been made.

The day was spent in all manner of gaiety. People walked all over the place, and admired the cedar lion, and bear, and giraffe, and colossal man, and, most of all, the fountain which changed its form every five minutes. In the pond beneath swam beautiful swans, while gazelles fled timidly about, and storks stood, as usual, like soldiers who had come back from the war with one leg. It would be impossible to repeat what everybody said and thought.

The evening was even finer. There were fireworks, Chinese lanterns, and fire-balloons, with the fountain playing all the time. The guests were well placed, a band of music played for them, and the poor people were in the distance. Everyone was delighted. Rockets and Roman candles, and pinwheels followed so rapidly and were so brilliant, that people got tired of saying "Oh!" The last piece was the most magnificent. It was a battle piece. Six frigates appeared, and fired fireworks at each other; the cannon boomed, the rockets went off in every direction, and at last the ships all burned up together. After a great explosion, the red, green, and blue lights went out, and it was as black as it could be. The fountain, too, stopped, and the day was over.

It was soon perfectly still also; for as soon as the fireworks <u>ceased</u>, everyone left the grounds. Yet a few remained; there was life there yet. Two hens, who had each stayed to see the fireworks, came upon one another as they were going by different ways to the barnyard. One was black, the other was yellow, and so we distinguish them, for otherwise they had no names.

"What! You here?" exclaimed Black, who naturally saw the other first. "This is rather late to be out."

"The same to you," rejoined Yellow. "For my part I rather enjoy this fine night, though it certainly is somewhat dark. I had no idea that night was quite so black."

"But it was bright enough just now," said the other. "That was a fine show."

"Very!" said Yellow; "But, neighbor, let us not stand here. If you are on your way to the house, as I presume you are, let us go in company." So they walked on together, much to the relief of each.

"Yes, it was a superb show," resumed Yellow; "something unusual. I never saw anything so magnificent. John came into the house one night with two lanterns to look for eggs, and almost blinded us, but that was nothing to this."

"I suppose all the world was there," said Black; "I didn't count, but made a rough guess. No one would miss such a sight. It probably only happens once."

"Yes," said Yellow, "it is precisely like our golden egg," and she sighed, "once, and only once. The rich man has done it, and the world may now stop."

"I suppose there could be nothing grander done," observed Black.

"You may be sure of that. It was no common thing. We go on laying eggs every day, but they are nothing but shell eggs. The rich man has been round the globe, and when he comes home you don't think he would settle down like people, and just mind his business! That would be laying shell eggs only. No, he lays the golden egg, depend upon it." The yellow hen, who prided herself on her wisdom, would have gone on much longer upon the subject of eggs, but at this moment there was a rustling in the bushes.

"The fire-sticks are all down, I hope," whispered Black. "I dodged about when they fell before"; but as she spoke, the Stork stepped in a dignified manner on the gravel walk, and approached them.

"Good evening," said Yellow, in a faint voice, and Black tried to say the same; the Stork took no notice of them, but Yellow, seeing more distinctly who it was, and being anxious to talk, stopped her walk, and continued. "I was just saying to my friend how fine it was tonight. We are fortunate in living in such times. Nothing like it ever known before. The golden egg, no doubt." I have a theory, that hens always come round to this point, and Yellow would have now come around to it again, but the Stork interrupted her.

"When you have seen as much of the world as I have, you will change your mind. Eggs!" and the Stork drew himself up on one leg; "Eggs! There is something better to be done. The rich man is a fool. Let him stand on one leg and think, instead of burning his fingers with matches. To find out what we are made of and what is to come of it—that is the only thing," and he walked away.

"Just hear him!" said Black. "Suppose we see what we are made of. But I can't understand. Can you?"

"Yes, but it's not easy to explain," said Yellow, and they talked no more. Yet they listened, for they were passing through the cedar trees. Conversation was there going on there.

"Say what you will," said the colossal man, "it is very fine to look like a man."

It was to an elm that he spoke, and the elm replied, "I think you have lost your good sense, friend, since the gardener trimmed you. You were very contented then, and had no foolish thoughts."

"Foolish thoughts! I think of the fireworks, and the fountain, and the music, as the rich man does. Don't speak of those old days when I was in low society."

"Is this anything like a roar?" said the cedar lion, rubbing his branches. "I think I made a pretty good lion."

"In time! In time!" said the cedar bear. "I believe my business is to growl, what do you say to this?" and he growled as he thought.

"It is extraordinary how tall I am," said the cedar giraffe. "This is living to some purpose. I really never knew before what I could be."

"Just hear them all!" said the elm to a neighbor. "I thought they would have been too ashamed to speak, and yet they now despise us. We are only trees, they tell us. Well, I am content. It is good enough for me. Here I have grown, and what I shall come to I can't say, but something fine, no doubt. So, neighbor, I think the best we can do is to grow."

"How will that do?" asked the black hen.

"I think we had best keep on laying eggs," said Yellow. "Perhaps the golden one will turn up after all; who knows?" And they walked on to the barn, where they had to stay outside till morning.

The trees now were also silent, for steps were heard. Two friends, an artist and a poet, out of the crowd of guests, were walking past, enjoying the quiet. They walked to another part of the grounds, away from the still fountain, and the tortured trees, and the blackened fireworks.

"Here are some trees one might paint," said the artist, looking around with admiration upon some oaks. "Those cedars! Good for firewood. But an oak looks well in a picture. By the way, that would have been a fine night-scene to paint—the fireworks lighting up the crowd of poor people on the grass—a pretty scene; it had good points."

"The heavens make the most splendid display of fire," said the poet, looking up. "Let us walk here all night, and watch the changes of the sky and see how we are affected—what thoughts we have, and then I can put it down in verse." Then they talked of nature, art, unity, and the poetic soul, but no one wants to listen to such talk. Indeed, they tired of it soon, and passed out of the gate, somewhat sleepy. It was the gate out of which the poor people went; but all had not gone.

Under the trees still walked two of these. They also had seen the fireworks, and they had seen the trees and the stars, but they had better things to talk of.

"I would not exchange all this for you," said he.

"Well," said she, "if it were yours I do not think I should love you more."

1. Why had it been a long time since the rich man had seen his house?

     ___ A. He had been traveling outside the country.
     ___ B. He had been working and did not pay much attention to his house.
     ___ C. He had been living in his city house.
     ___ D. He had been staying with family in another country.

2. In paragraph 6 the guests sigh to themselves, "What a tame country ours is!" This suggests that the guests feel

     ___ A. that the rich man was truly a wise man.
     ___ B. that things must be wild and dangerous abroad.
     ___ C. that things must be so much more exciting abroad.
     ___ D. that the rich man is probably not telling the truth.

3. Why did the rich man want the poor people to attend his festival?

     ___ A. so that they would envy his great wealth
     ___ B. because he wanted to give them something wonderful to remember
     ___ C. because he thought their presence would add to the beauty of the scene
     ___ D. because he himself was once a poor man

4. In paragraph 13, the author states, "… for as soon as the fireworks ceased, everyone left the grounds." A synonym for ceased is

     ___ A. explained.
     ___ B. began.
     ___ C erupted.
     ___ D. stopped.

5. Why did the author name one of the hens Black and the other one Yellow?

     ___ A. He didn't know their real names.
     ___ B. They did not have names so the author made them up.
     ___ C. Those were their nicknames.
     ___ D. One of the hens was covered in ashes from the fireworks.

6. Why does the yellow hen say that she will just keep laying eggs?

     ___ A. The more eggs a hen lays the better.
     ___ B. You never know when the golden one will turn up.
     ___ C. It is a hen's job to lay as many eggs as she can.
     ___ D. The yellow hen is foolish and has nothing better to do.

7. What effect did changing their shape have on the cedar trees?

     ___ A. They felt lonely since the other trees would have nothing to do with them.
     ___ B. They began to behave like the creatures they were made to resemble.
     ___ C. They were embarrassed that their natural beauty had been destroyed.
     ___ D. They were frightened that they would soon become firewood.

8. How did the poet and the artist view the rich man's gardens and fireworks display?

     ___ A. They were inspired to write about the beauty the rich man had created.
     ___ B. They envied the rich man for his great wealth and beautiful possessions.
     ___ C. They felt the rich man wasted his money on "things" when he could help the poor.
     ___ D. They preferred natural surroundings to the rich man's decorations and displays.

9. In this story you learn about the different personalities of the characters by what they are saying about the day's events. Compare the personalities of the hens with that of the stork.

_____

_____

_____

_____

_____

_____

_____

_____

_____

_____

_____

_____

_____

_____

_____

10. Below is a semantic map of the rich man from *The Rich Man's Place* and a list of words that can be used to describe him. Read the list of words and choose the five words that best describe him.

You may use words from the box or you may use your own words. Write these words on the lines provided. The first one has been done for you.

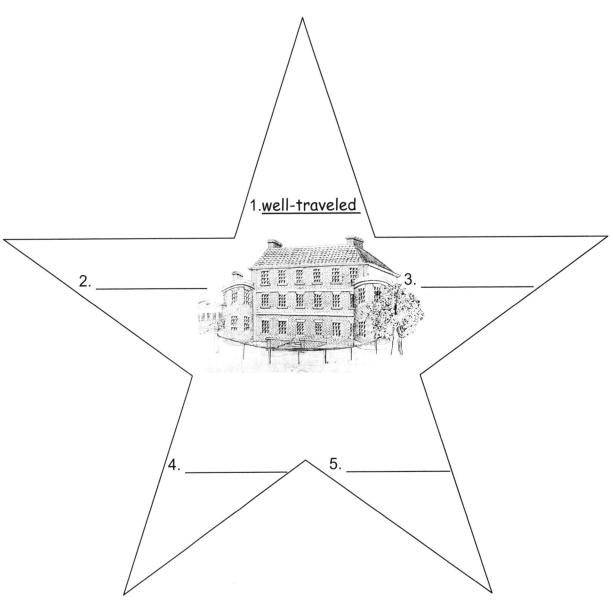

1. well-traveled

2. _____

3. _____

4. _____

5. _____

Word List			
artistic	educated	proud	mean
generous	boastful	humble	jealous
materialistic	fearless	foolish	unhappy
greedy	~~well-traveled~~	talented	lonely

The Brave Tin Soldier
by Hans Christian Anderson

There were twenty-five tin soldiers. All were brothers, for they had been made from the same tin kitchen spoon. They stood shoulder to shoulder and looked straight ahead, and they looked very smart in their red and blue uniforms. The first thing they heard, when the lid of their box was removed was, "Tin Soldiers!" which was yelled by a little boy, who clapped his hands. They were given to him as a birthday present. As he began to set them up on the table, he noticed that they were all exactly alike, except for one. He was different for he had only one leg; he was the last to be molded and there was not enough tin left. Yet he stood just as well on one leg as the others did on two, and he is this story's hero!

On the table where they were set, there were many other toys. The one which everyone looked at and admired most was an exquisite paper castle. You could see right through its little windows, into the tiny little rooms. The front yard had little trees and shrubs that were perfectly arranged around a small piece of mirror which was intended to look like a lake. Swans molded out of wax appeared to float effortlessly across its surface as they looked down and gazed at their <u>reflections</u>. Their feathers were as white as new fallen snow.

There was a girl who stood in the open doorway; she too was cut of paper. Her arms were stretched out and one of her legs was raised so high in the air that the tin soldier could not see it at all, and he thought that she too had only one leg.

"She would be the perfect partner for me," he thought. "But she is talented and she lives in a castle, and I only live in a small box. I will still try to make her acquaintance." He lay down behind a small box on the table so the boy would not see him when he picked up his toys before bed.

When nighttime came, all of his brothers were put away in their box, and the little boy went to bed. This was the time when the toys began to engage in games of their own. The twenty-five soldiers rattled around in their box, for they too wanted to play with the other toys, but they couldn't get the lid off their box. The toys were having a fine time visiting with one another and running around on the table. The only two who didn't move at all were the tin soldier and the little dancer; she continued to stand on the point of her toe, with her arms stretched out; he stood at attention on his single tin leg.

As the clock struck twelve, the lid of a small toy box flew open and out hopped a little goblin. There was no jack-in-the-box in the box; it was a kind of trick. "Tin soldier!" yelled the goblin. "Keep your eyes to yourself!"

The tin soldier continued to stand at attention and pretended not to hear.

"Wait until tomorrow! You'll be sorry!" screeched the goblin.

When morning arrived and the children were up again, the tin soldier was set upon the windowsill. The goblin may have been responsible, or perhaps the wind; the window suddenly flew open, and

out flew the tin soldier. He fell three stories down to the ground below. It was a terrible fall! His leg pointed upwards, his head was down, and he came to a halt with his bayonet stuck between the paving stones.

The little girl and the little boy went to search for him in the street but they couldn't find him. If he had called out, "Here I am!" they would have found him easily, but he didn't think it was proper behavior to cry out when he was in uniform.

It began to rain and the drops fell quickly. It was a drenching shower; rivers of water formed in the streets. When it was over two children passed. "Look!" said one of them. "There's a tin soldier. He should have a boat to sail in. Let's put him out to sea."

So they made a boat out of newspaper and put the soldier in the middle, and set it in the fast-flowing gutter at the edge of the street. Away he sped, and the two children ran beside him clapping their hands. What waves there were in the gutter-stream, what rolling tides! It had been a real downpour. The paper boat tossed up and down, and sometimes whirled around and around. The soldier felt quite sick. But he remained as <u>steadfast</u> as ever, not moving a muscle, still looking straight in front of him.

12

Suddenly, the boat entered a tunnel under the pavement. Oh, it was dark! "Wherever am I going now?" the tin soldier wondered. "Yes, it must have been the goblin's doing. Oh! If only the paper dancer were here with me in the boat, I wouldn't care about anything else."

All at once, from its home in the tunnel, out rushed a large water rat. "Have you a passport?" it demanded. "No admittance without a passport."

But the tin soldier never said a word; he only gripped his musket more tightly than ever. The boat rushed onwards, and behind it rushed the rat. He yelled, "Stop him! Stop him! He hasn't paid his toll! He hasn't shown his passport!"

How could he stop? He was already too close to the edge. The boat raced on, and the poor tin soldier held himself as stiffly as he could.

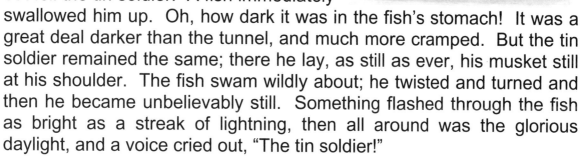

Suddenly, the little boat swirled around four times and filled with water right up to the brim; what could it do but sink! The tin soldier stood in water up to his neck, deeper and deeper sank the boat, and softer and softer grew the paper, until at last the water came over the soldier's head. He thought of the little dancer whom he would never see again, and he sang this song:

Onward, warrior brave,
Drifting onward to thy grave.

The paper boat fell to pieces and out fell the tin soldier. A fish immediately swallowed him up. Oh, how dark it was in the fish's stomach! It was a great deal darker than the tunnel, and much more cramped. But the tin soldier remained the same; there he lay, as still as ever, his musket still at his shoulder. The fish swam wildly about; he twisted and turned and then he became unbelievably still. Something flashed through the fish as bright as a streak of lightning, then all around was the glorious daylight, and a voice cried out, "The tin soldier!"

The fish had been caught by a fisherman, taken to market, sold and carried into the kitchen, where the cook had cut it open with a large carving knife. Now she picked up the soldier, held him around his waist between her finger and thumb, and took him into the living room, so that the family could see the remarkable character who had traveled about inside a fish, but the tin soldier was not at all proud of this. They stood him up on the table and there he saw the same room where his adventures had begun; there were the very same children; there were the very same toys. And there was the fine paper castle with the graceful little dancer standing at the door; she was still poised on one leg, with the other raised high in the air and she stood as firm as the tin soldier. The tin soldier was deeply moved, he would have liked to weep tin tears, only that would not have been soldierly behavior. He looked at her, and she looked at him, but not a word passed between them.

Suddenly one of the little children took the tin soldier and threw him into the stove. He had no reason for doing this; it must have been the fault of the goblin that lived in the little toy box. The flame lighted up the tin soldier, as he stood. The heat was terrible, but whether this came from the fire or his burning love, he could not tell. The bright colors were faded from his uniform, whether they were washed away from his journey or his grief, no one could say. He looked at the little dancer, and she looked at him; he felt that he was melting away, but he remained firm with his musket at his shoulder. Suddenly the door flew open and a gust of air caught the paper dancer, and she fluttered like a butterfly into the

stove by the side of the tin soldier. Instantly the flames, the tin soldier, and the dancer were gone.

The soldier melted down to a lump of tin, and the next day, when the cook raked the ashes out of the stove, she found him in the shape of a little tin heart. But of the little dancer nothing remained of her but a bead from her dress, and that was as black as soot.

1. Why is the story called *The Brave Tin Soldier*?

   ___ A. The tin soldier remains brave throughout the different problems
   he faces in the story.
   ___ B. The tin soldier has only one leg and, therefore, he is
   handicapped, so he must be very brave.
   ___ C. The cook is proud of the tin soldier for surviving in the fish's
   stomach, so she brings him to show the others.
   ___ D. The tin soldier is the only soldier who dares to hide behind the
   little box so that the boy will not put him away at the end of the
   day.

2. *The Brave Tin Soldier* is a

   ___ A. mystery.
   ___ B. fairy tale.
   ___ C. biography.
   ___ D. fable.

3. Where did the tin to make the tin soldiers come from?

   ___ A. a tin spoon
   ___ B. a tin fork
   ___ C. a toy store
   ___ D. a birthday gift

4. In paragraph 2, the author writes, "Swans molded out of wax appeared to
   float effortlessly across the surface as they looked down and gazed at
   their <u>reflections</u>." What is the best synonym for <u>reflections</u>?

   ___ A. water
   ___ B. retreats
   ___ C. differences
   ___ D. images

5. Why did the soldier think that the paper dancer would be a perfect partner for him?

     __ A. because they had both been given as birthday presents
     __ B. because they were both good dancers
     __ C. because he thought she had only one leg, like he did
     __ D. because she was beautiful

6. In paragraph 12, the author writes, "But he remained as <u>steadfast</u> as ever, not moving a muscle, still looking straight in front of him." What does the word steadfast mean in this sentence?

     __ A. firm
     __ B. frightened
     __ C. dry
     __ D. lonely

7. In paragraph 22 the author writes, "Suddenly the door flew open and a gust of air caught the paper dancer, and she fluttered like a butterfly into the stove by the side of the tin soldier." This means the dancer

     __ A. danced happily into the fire.
     __ B. turned into a butterfly.
     __ C. flew into a trap set by the goblin.
     __ D. flew gracefully into the fire.

8. Which character is the villain in this story?

     __ A. the tin soldier
     __ B. the paper dancer
     __ C. the goblin
     __ D. the cook

9. Some people would call the tin soldier handicapped because he has only one leg. The author calls him the story's hero. Do you agree or disagree? Do you think the story would have had a different ending if the tin soldier were not handicapped?

_____

_____

_____

_____

_____

_____

_____

_____

_____

_____

_____

_____

_____

_____

10. Below is a graphic organizer for the story *The Brave Tin Soldier*. Think about the story and recall the important events in the order that they happened. Write the events in the boxes provided.

FIRST:

NEXT:

NEXT:

LAST:

Exercise 1

Endangered Species Problem

The number of people on this earth has grown, and wildlife habitats have been destroyed. Many animals have lost their homes and are at risk of becoming extinct. In fact, some animals have already become extinct. This means they will never live on this earth again. Pollution and hunting continue to place many animals at risk. However, loss of habitat is the main problem.

Habitat loss and extinction of entire species hurt people. Plants and animals provide many benefits to humans. Many medicines come from nature. For example, the Houston toad makes substances that are being studied for use in the prevention of heart attacks. This species is almost extinct because of habitat loss. The prescription drug makers count on nature for success. Many of the top 150 prescribed drugs have come from nature. Survival of animals and plants is important.

The main way for protecting species is the Endangered Species Act (ESA). It was passed by Congress in 1973 to protect over 1,000 different species by making it illegal to hunt or destroy endangered animals, and to set aside land as refuge for these animals. Hundreds of species that used to be in trouble have improved because of protections offered under the ESA. Animals in danger are placed on a list. They are listed either as threatened or endangered. Those at greater risk of extinction are listed as endangered.

Concerned people can make a difference. The people at the National Wildlife Federation are working every day to help endangered species. Learning about endangered species is important. People telling other people about endangered species may help save those species at risk.

The following eight animals are listed as either threatened or endangered.

Gray Wolf

In the U.S., the gray wolf lives mostly in the Midwest and in Alaska. Once, it could be found almost everywhere in North America. Before being given ESA protection, wolves were killed by ranchers and farmers. Today the greatest threat to the wolf is people who continue to hunt it. Education can help save the wolf. The gray wolf in America is beginning to make a comeback.

Grizzly Bear

The grizzly bear once roamed the entire western half of North America. Now there are only 900 to 1,000 grizzlies left in the lower 48 states. About 35,000 grizzlies live in Alaska and 22,000 in Canada. The main threat to the grizzly bear is habitat destruction. As trees and forests are cut down, the grizzly bear has fewer places to live. People also continue to hunt grizzlies. The most important way to help the grizzly bear is to save what is left of its habitat.

Florida Panther

The Florida panther lives only in Florida. It is one of the most endangered species on Earth. There are only 30 to 50 Florida panthers left in the wild. Road kills on Florida's highways are a major cause of death. Road building and water projects have left parts of its habitat too dry. Loss of habitat due to building is also a problem. Now, public lands have been set aside as panther preserves.

Utah Prairie Dog

The Utah prairie dog lives in southwest Utah. The Utah prairie dog is the size of a squirrel. It spends its days playing, eating grass and calling to other prairie dogs. Coyotes, foxes, badgers, hawks, and eagles attack prairie dogs. However, the main threat to the Utah prairie dog is ranchers and farmers who think it is a pest and poison it. Even though it is now listed as threatened in Utah, the killings continue. Public education will help save the remaining prairie dogs.

Sonoran Pronghorn

The Sonoran pronghorn lives in Arizona and Mexico. The pronghorn can run as fast as 50 mph. The main threat to the pronghorn is habitat destruction and drought. In addition, hunting has also wiped out many pronghorns. The pronghorn now receives almost complete protection in the U.S. It is hoped that this protection and good rainfall will help the pronghorn recover.

Canadian Lynx

The Canadian lynx lives in Canada, Alaska, and in some northern U.S. states. Lynx populations are still fairly healthy in Canada and Alaska, but it has almost disappeared in the U.S. The main threat to the lynx is habitat destruction. It requires large areas that are free of humans. Hunting and over-trapping have also reduced its numbers. For the lynx to recover in the U.S., large wooded areas will have to be protected. The lynx is not protected by the Endangered Species Act, but may be in the near future.

Red-cockaded Woodpecker

The red-cockaded woodpecker lives in forests in the southeastern U.S. and eastern Texas. It is a small bird. It hunts insects in trees. It depends on old pine forests to survive. Habitat destruction is the main threat facing this bird. Poisonous chemicals used in the forest are also a problem. Some of these wood-peckers are beginning to increase in number. The most important way to help it is to protect forestlands.

Bald Eagle

The bald eagle is making a terrific comeback. It is no longer listed as endangered but as threatened. In fact, it may be taken off the list in the near future. It lives in the lower 48 states of the U.S., Alaska, and Canada. The chemical DDT was the main danger to the bald eagle in the early 1970s. Since then, DDT has been banned. Habitat destruction remains a problem. However, the bald eagle is a success story of the Endangered Species Act.

1. Suppose you were selecting pictures of threatened or endangered animals for your class display board. Which of the following questions would not affect your decision on choosing which animal to display?

    __ A. What kind of pet would this animal make?
    __ B. What can people do to help this animal?
    __ C. What have people done to harm this animal?
    __ D. What is the main threat to this animal?

2. If you did not know the meaning of the word habitat, what clue would help you figure it out?

    __ A. Certain animals need protection from hunters.
    __ B. Poisonous chemicals are a problem.
    __ C. Many animals have lost their homes.
    __ D. The woodpecker hunts insects in trees.

3. Which is the greatest threat to most endangered species?

    __ A. drought
    __ B. forest fire
    __ C. habitat destruction
    __ D. pollution

4. Which endangered animal might a rancher or farmer be reluctant to help increase in number?

    __ A. Canadian Lynx
    __ B. Utah Prairie Dog
    __ C. Grizzly Bear
    __ D. Bald Eagle

5. Compared to threatened species, an endangered species is

    ___ A. more valuable to humans.
    ___ B. more likely to become extinct.
    ___ C. protected by law.
    ___ D. more harmful to people.

6. Which of the animals listed in the article might be found in New Jersey?

    ___ A. Sonoran Pronghorn
    ___ B. Red-cockaded Woodpecker
    ___ C. Gray Wolf
    ___ D. Bald Eagle

7. According to the article, "Lynx populations are still fairly healthy in Canada and Alaska, but it has almost disappeared in the U.S." Which of the following is the most likely reason for the disappearance of the animal in the U.S.?

    ___ A. The Canadian lynx prefers a colder climate.
    ___ B. There is more development and habitat destruction in the U.S.
    ___ C. The people in Alaska and Canada are doing more to help save the animal.
    ___ D. There are more hunters in the U.S.

8. Why is the bald eagle likely to be taken off the threatened species list in the near future?

    ___ A. because it is being reclassified as an endangered species
    ___ B. because it is the symbol of our country
    ___ C. because the number of bald eagles is increasing
    ___ D. because it will soon be extinct

9. Should all endangered species be protected by law, or just certain ones? Explain why you feel this way. Use information from the article to support your opinion.

_____

_____

_____

_____

_____

_____

_____

_____

_____

_____

_____

_____

_____

_____

10. Choose one of the eight species listed in the article. Use the information given to complete the chart below.

Name of endangered animal.

Where can it be found?

The dangers it faces.

What can be done to save it?

Places of Interest in New Jersey

New Jersey is a state rich in history and culture. From High Point Monument in the north to Cape May Light House in the south, there are attractions for all ages. There are state parks, sports complexes, amusement parks, ski resorts and sandy beaches. Here are just a few places to see when you visit the southern part of the Garden State.

Barnegat Lighthouse State Park is located at Barnegat Light on the northern tip of Long Beach Island. The park has areas where park visitors can picnic, sunbathe, fish, bird watch, and visit the lighthouse. There is a beautiful path along the ocean for walking and fishing.

The original Barnegat Lighthouse was a 40-foot brick tower constructed in 1834. Due to erosion the lighthouse toppled into the sea in 1856. A temporary wooden structure was built while the current Barnegat Lighthouse was being constructed. "Old Barney" was first lighted on January 1, 1858, and performed its duties for 69 years until it was decommissioned in 1927.

 The U.S. Coast Guard used the lighthouse as a lookout tower during World War II. At the end of the war, the lighthouse and its surrounding property were turned over to the State and opened as a State Park in 1958.

The red and white marvel is approximately 175 feet tall and has 217 steps to the top. At the top, visitors may step outside for a walk around the watch gallery for spectacular views of Barnegat Inlet, Island Beach State Park, and Long Beach Island. The interior of the lighthouse is open 9:00 A.M. to 4:30 P.M. May through October. The lighthouse is open weekends from November to April 9:00 A.M. to 3:30 P.M. On selected evenings throughout the summer the lighthouse will be open until 9:30 P.M. to see the sunset over Barnegat Bay or the moonrise over the Atlantic Ocean.

The Brigantine Wilderness Area, once a separate wildlife sanctuary, is now part of the Edwin B. Forsythe National Wildlife Refuge. In 1984, the Brigantine Refuge was combined with the Barnegat division under the Edwin B. Forsythe name, in honor of the late congressman from New Jersey.

Almost 90 percent of the Forsythe Refuge is tidal salt meadow and marsh, combined with shallow coves and bays. These lands provide important resting and feeding habitat for water birds. A large amount of marsh vegetation provides important food and cover for many types of wildlife.

Visitors to the refuge may enjoy a wide range of wildlife related activities. An 8-mile drive through a variety of wetland and upland habitats and two short foot trails provide excellent opportunities to view wildlife. The Edwin B. Forsythe NWR is also ideal as an outdoor classroom for environmental education where students can spot great blue herons, giant swans, glossy ibis, and other kinds of birds.

Fantasy Island Amusement Park

Fantasy Island Amusement Park is located in Beach Haven near the southern tip of Long Beach Island. It features live entertainment, a family arcade, a miniature golf course, rides, games, prizes, food and an ice-cream parlor. There are also batting cages and a waterslide area.

The park is open daily from the end of June to the end of August and on weekends from Mid-May to Mid-June. The amusement park is closed the rest of the year.

Fridays are POP (pay one price) days. Ride all the rides for one low price from the time the park opens at 2:00 P.M. until 7:00 P.M. Regular prices are in effect from 7:00 P.M. until the park closes between 11:00 P.M. and midnight.

Batsto Village is located in Wharton State Forest, the site of a former bog iron and glass-making community. The Batsto Iron Works was founded in 1766 by famous Ironmaster Charles Reed and constructed on the banks of

the Batsto River. The complex was purchased by Joseph Wharton in 1876. Wharton built a sawmill, planted cranberries and other crops, and ran a forest products and agricultural business until his death in 1909. The State of New Jersey purchased Batsto in 1954. Today it is the center of the Wharton State Forest and is part of the Pinelands National Reserve.

Visitors can tour Batsto's more than 40 sites and buildings for a look into the 19th century world. Guided tours through Batsto Mansion are available throughout the year. There is also a Visitor Center, a 19th century ore boat, a charcoal kiln exhibit, ice and milk houses, a carriage house and stable, blacksmith and wheelwright shop, a gristmill, and a general store and post office that is still in operation.

Batsto Village is open daily 9:00 A.M. to 4:30 P.M. There is a full-time naturalist on staff who conducts national history programs for school groups.

Island Beach State Park, a 10-mile white-sand strip, is one of the few remaining natural barrier beaches on the Atlantic Coast. It is located in Seaside Park in Ocean County. Over 240 different birds have been spotted here including the peregrine falcon, brown pelican, and blue heron.

Visitors can enjoy many activities including swimming, sunbathing, surf fishing, scuba diving, crabbing, bird watching, nature trails, and nature tours conducted by park naturalists. Be sure to visit the nature museum and interpretive center when you visit.

The park is open year-round from 8:00 A.M. to 8:00 P.M. from Memorial Day through Labor Day.

Jenkinson's Aquarium is located on the boardwalk in Point Pleasant Beach. Exhibits on sharks, coral reefs, penguins, alligators, and seals allow visitors the opportunity to see up close animals from around the globe. The touch tank even allows visitors to touch live animals such as a sea star and a

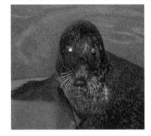

juvenile shark. In addition to its educational exhibits, the aquarium offers workshops for children of all ages and professional development workshops for teachers. Group tours for schools and scout troops are available.

The aquarium is open year-round, except holidays.

Popcorn Park Zoo is a federally-licensed refuge for wildlife, exotic and farm animals that need rescuing, protection and medical care. Since such animals cannot be released back to the wild, they are given homes at the zoo. It is located on seven acres in Forked River. There are currently over

200 animals and birds in the zoo. Among them are lions, tigers, black bears, monkeys, cougars, bobcats, deer, wallabies, reptiles, foxes, goats, horses, cows, peacocks, vultures, llamas, and many others. There is a picnic area for our guests, and cold drinks and ice cream are available.

The zoo is open 365 days a year, 11:00 A.M. to 5:00 P.M. except on holidays.

The <u>New Jersey State Aquarium</u>, located in Camden, is a multi-media complex that allows visitors to become part of the undersea world. They begin their tour in the Ocean Base Command Center and then it's on to the Shark Zone, the Coral Station, Mangrove Lagoon, Caribbean Beach and Pier, R.M.S. Rhone, Sea TV, Drama of the Delaware, and the 760,000-gallon Open Ocean Tank. Other exhibits include a 120-seat ampitheater, Sea Lab research station, and the Newt Suit one-man sub.

The aquarium features many hands-on exhibits, games, and puzzles that unlock the mysteries of the ocean. It has a full schedule of activities every day including performances by divers, seals, sharks, and snakes.

Throughout the year a variety of special events—fireworks, concerts, ice-sculpting, fishing demonstrations, and much more—give visitors great reasons to return.

The aquarium is open daily 9:30 A.M. to 5:30 P.M. April 16 to September 15. The rest of the year it is open 9:30 A.M. to 4:30 P.M. on weekdays and 10:00 A.M. to 5:00 P.M. on weekends.

<u>The Wonder Museum</u> is an interactive children's museum with more than 50 hands-on activities. Visitors can learn about history, geography, science, culture, and different occupations. Exhibits include an explorer ship modeled after Columbus' ship the *Pinta*, Dinosaur Valley, a 22' high teepee, a

single-seat biplane, a frontier cabin, a TV studio, a medieval castle, a moon landing, and critter country. Children can see a real meteorite or climb aboard a model-T, an ambulance, and a fire engine. There are also computer facilities, a dance studio, arts and crafts, a music room, a theater, a construction site, a magnetic circus, and much more.

The museum is open daily except for Easter, Thanksgiving, Christmas, and New Year's Day. Hours are 10:00 A.M. to 6:00 P.M. Monday through Saturday, and 10:00 A.M. to 5:00 P.M. on Sunday.

1. The author writes that Barnegat Lighthouse "was <u>decommissioned</u> in 1927." Based on context clues, what is the best definition for <u>decommissioned</u>?

    ___ A. torn down
    ___ B. taken out of service
    ___ C. rebuilt
    ___ D. moved to another place

2. Which of these places is <u>not</u> open during the winter months?

    ___ A. Barnegat Lighthouse
    ___ B. Batsto Village
    ___ C. Fantasy Island Amusement Park
    ___ D. The Wonder Museum

3. Suppose you are planning a trip on a cool, cloudy, summer day. Which of the following questions could you ask to help you decide on a good place to visit?

    ___ A. What time does the attraction close for the day?
    ___ B. Are there picnic facilities on the grounds?
    ___ C. Are there indoor activities available?
    ___ D. Is there any admission fee charged?

4. What is the best place to visit if you are interested in learning historic information?

    ___ A. The Brigantine Wilderness Area
    ___ B. Popcorn Park Zoo
    ___ C. Batsto Village
    ___ D. Jenkinson's Aquarium

5. The Brigantine Wilderness Area and the Popcorn Park Zoo are two examples of a wildlife <u>refuge</u>. A <u>refuge</u> is a place where animals

    ___ A. are raised for food.
    ___ B. are sold as pets.
    ___ C. are protected.
    ___ D. perform for visitors.

6. According to the article, Edwin B. Forsythe was

    __ A. governor of New Jersey.
    __ B. a famous naturalist.
    __ C. a famous ironmaster.
    __ D. a congressman from New Jersey.

7. If you go to Fantasy Island Amusement Park on Friday and buy the POP (pay-one-price) admission, how long can you stay at the park?

    __ A. until 7:00 P.M. when the park closes
    __ B. until midnight, and all rides are included in the POP price
    __ C. until midnight, but you must pay for all rides after 7:00 P.M.
    __ D. until 7:00 P.M. when you must pay for another POP admission

8. In what section of the newspaper would you most likely find an article about the Brigantine Wilderness Area?

    __ A. the local news
    __ B. the sports section
    __ C. the travel section
    __ D. the editorial section

9. Which of the following places of interest is not owned by the state of New Jersey?

    __ A. Barnegat Lighthouse
    __ B. Batsto Village
    __ C. Island Beach State Park
    __ D. Popcorn Park Zoo

10. What would be another good title for this article?

    __ A. New Jersey is for the Birds and Other Wildlife
    __ B. What to Do When You Visit New Jersey
    __ C. A Guide to State Parks in New Jersey
    __ D. Where to Go on Your Next Class Trip

11. Pick the two places described in this article that you would most like to visit. Explain why you chose these two places.

_____

_____

_____

_____

_____

_____

_____

_____

_____

_____

_____

_____

_____

_____

_____

_____

_____

_____

_____

_____

_____

_____

_____

_____

_____

_____

_____

_____

Below is a map that shows several points of interest along the New Jersey shore. Examine the map and answer the questions.

12. If someone living in Philadelphia wanted to visit Cape May, what two highways should he or she take?

___ A. 78 and Atlantic City Expressway
___ B. 80 and Garden State Parkway
___ C. Atlantic City Expressway and Garden State Parkway
___ D. 95 and Garden State Parkway

13. In which direction would you travel if you wanted to go from Seaside Park to Sandy Hook?

___ A. north
___ B. south
___ C. east
___ D. west

14. According to the map, what attraction is at the southern-most point of New Jersey?

___ A. Seaside Park
___ B. Cape May
___ C. Wildwood
___ D. Sandy Hook

The Little Theatre of the Deaf

About 35 years ago a very unique type of theatrical performance was created by David Hays, a theatrical director, who was inspired by well known psychologist and author, Dr. Edna Levine, to form the National Theatre of the Deaf. This unique <u>ensemble</u> of deaf and hearing entertainers has brought laughter and tears to people all over the world. They perform for audiences of all ages. The deaf actors use an extremely visual style to tell stories that combine the elements of voice, body movement, facial expression, mime, and sign language—all blended into an artistic whole.

The Little Theatre of the Deaf, the children's wing of the National Theatre of the Deaf, is comprised of two traveling troupes that perform for elementary school age children and their parents, in schools, city parks, libraries, museums, and theaters around the world.

Each troupe is made up of five performers, four deaf and one hearing. They usually begin their program with a short introduction that acquaints the audience with sign language, the visual language of the deaf community.

Sign language consists of formal hand movements for specific words and concepts, or ideas. Names and words that do not have formal signs can be finger-spelled. Each letter of the alphabet has a corresponding hand shape, and words can be spelled in the air using the various hand shapes. After the introduction the actual performance of the deaf actors begins. The audience sees the words they've just learned used in context, and they understand more fully how much fun it is to watch stories performed in sign language. The sign language vocabulary is also included in the program guide given to each person in the audience at the beginning of the performance.

The Little Theatre of the Deaf's theatrical performances include a number of short stories, fables, fairy tales, and poems. The actors and actresses tell stories without sound or musical accompaniment, using only body movements and facial expressions, intertwined with formal sign language. The hearing member of the troupe narrates what is being said by the deaf actors.

The *Giving Tree* is the centerpiece of each performance by The Little Theatre of the Deaf. "Once there was a tree...." so begins a story of unforgettable perception, which offers the gift of giving and unconditional love, beautifully written by the talented Shelley Silverstein.

Concluding each performance of the deaf actors is a popular interactive improvisational piece called "Your Game." The audience suggests objects they want the actors to become, and the performers use their bodies to create monkeys, washing machines, chairs, and other objects. The actors work together to create intricate objects.

Millions of children have been exposed to the beauty and grace of sign language on television all over the world. Many actors who started their careers at the Little Theatre of the Deaf have become famous later for their performances on television programs such as Sesame Street and movies such as *Children of a Lesser God* and *Love is Never Silent*.

The National Theatre of the Deaf, the parent company of the Little Theatre of the Deaf, has its home base at the Hazel E. Stark Center in Chester, Connecticut. Rehearsal space, classrooms, and theatrical shops are located there. Students can attend a concentrated five-week summer school which includes courses in basic and advanced theater study, acting, directing, playwriting, costume and set design, and other topics.

The company's performers do not spend much time at the center, except between tours. Since it was founded in 1967, the company has given over 5000 performances, touring all fifty states and internationally in Canada, Europe, Japan, India, Mexico, and China. The Little Theatre of the Deaf has delighted children with its magical performances and has brought new awareness and understanding of the deaf and their capabilities.

Sign language is now more readily accepted and practiced by the hearing community, thus decreasing the sense of isolation felt by deaf persons. In addition, job opportunities for deaf and hearing impaired persons in the theater, film, and television industries, as well as other areas once closed to the deaf—have broadened dramatically. All these accomplishments can be credited to the hard work and talented efforts of hundreds of deaf men and women fulfilling a dream.

1. The author's purpose for writing this article is to

    ___ A.   inform people that the deaf can become theatrical performers.
    ___ B.   explain how sign language works.
    ___ C.   create job opportunities for deaf people.
    ___ D.   emphasize accomplishments of disabled persons.

2. A synonym for the word <u>ensemble</u> in the first paragraph is

    ___ A.   deaf actor.
    ___ B.   party.
    ___ C.   group.
    ___ D.   school.

3. What activity would be more difficult for deaf persons to perform than for hearing persons?

    ___ A. climbing a mountain
    ___ B. ballet dancing
    ___ C. painting
    ___ D. running

4. If you had a deaf classmate and you didn't know sign language, how would you communicate?

    ___ A. raise your voice
    ___ B. write a note
    ___ C. smile
    ___ D. whisper

5. In addition to sign language, deaf and hard of hearing persons use other methods to communicate, except

    ___ A. email and instant messaging.
    ___ B. regular telephones.
    ___ C. writing notes on paper.
    ___ D. reading lips.

6. A mime uses hand gestures and body movements to

    ___ A. signal the start of a show.
    ___ B. tell a story.
    ___ C. get children in the audience to quiet down.
    ___ D. accompany musical performances.

7. The Little Theatre of the Deaf was formed to give deaf performers an opportunity to

    ___ A. travel around the world.
    ___ B. perform musical pieces.
    ___ C. entertain hearing audiences.
    ___ D. dance.

8. In this article the author tells us about the use of sign language to communicate with deaf persons. What other methods of communication could you use to "talk" with a deaf or hard of hearing classmate?

_____

_____

_____

_____

_____

_____

_____

_____

_____

_____

_____

_____

_____

_____

_____

_____

_____

_____

_____

_____

_____

9. Why do you think it is important for deaf children to learn sign language?

_____

_____

_____

_____

_____

_____

_____

_____

_____

_____

_____

_____

_____

_____

_____

_____

_____

_____

_____

_____

_____

_____

_____

_____

10. Why do deaf persons feel a sense of isolation? What are some of the ways a hearing person might help them overcome this feeling?

_____

_____

_____

_____

_____

_____

_____

_____

_____

_____

_____

_____

_____

_____

_____

_____

_____

_____

_____

_____

_____

_____

_____

Caring for Your New Dog

Feeding

A dog will eat most foods that people eat, but what it finds tasty is not always good for it. To keep your dog fit, it is best to buy food specially made for dogs. Make sure the food you buy is right for the age and size of your dog. If you are not sure which dog food to buy, ask your veterinarian to help you choose the right food for your dog.

<u>Nutritious foods</u>. Be sure to feed your dog a food that has all the necessary nutrients that he or she needs. Ask your veterinarian about which brands of dog food he or she recommends.

<u>Feeding times.</u> Give your puppy small meals three or four times a day. When it is older, it will only need one or two meals a day. It is easy to remember to feed your dog if you feed it just after you have your breakfast and your evening meal.

<u>How much to feed</u>. The label will tell you how much to feed your dog every day. You may need to know how heavy the dog is. If your dog gets chubby, give it less food. If you start to see its bones, you should ask your veterinarian for help. Always make sure your dog has a bowl of clean water. Without water, it will quickly become sick. Never give your dog milk, fruit juice, or soda.

Training Your Dog

Train your dog to remember those things you want it to do, such as to sit, to stay, or to fetch a ball. Dogs learn in a very simple way. If it's fun, it must be worth doing again! Start to train your dog as soon as you get it but keep the lessons short. Try a one-minute training session several times a day, and you'll be surprised to see what you both can do.

1. Teaching your dog to sit is easy. Each time it sits down, say the word "sit" slowly and clearly. Soon it will learn to sit each time you tell it to.

2. Now train your dog to stay when you walk away. Put your hand out flat toward the dog's face. Say

"stay" slowly. Then gradually take a few steps back, repeating "stay." If your dog follows you, begin again.

3. Next teach your dog to come to you when you call. Use a long leash until you are sure it will not run off. Bend down so it can see your eyes and wait a moment. Then call it, using his name and the word "come."

4. Your dog should sit at your feet when it comes to you. Make sure it doesn't jump up. A puppy leaping up to your face may be fun, but when it grows bigger, it could knock you over.

5. Praise your dog immediately whenever it does as it is asked. It does not have a long memory and soon forgets what it has just done. One of the best rewards is a plain old hug, or give it a food treat. Do not hit your dog if he misbehaves, rather stop playing with it or put it in its cage for a short time.

Grooming Your Dog

Your dog is covered in fur from its nose to the tip of its tail. The hairy coat helps keep it warm. The oil in your dog's coat prevents its skin from getting wet. You should groom your dog's fur every day to keep it clean and shiny.

If your dog has long hair, you will need a grooming brush and a wire comb with rounded prongs.

If your dog has short fur, you need a special rubber grooming glove to remove loose hair and dirt. You can get this grooming glove from your veterinarian or a pet store.

Praise your dog for being patient by giving it a big hug. If you always reward it, it will be happy to be groomed every day.

1. The author writes, "Be sure to feed your dog a food that has all the necessary <u>nutrients</u> that your dog needs." What are <u>nutrients</u>?

    ___ A. flavorings
    ___ B. vitamins and minerals
    ___ C. calories
    ___ D. meat

2. According to the article, the best way to train a dog is to

    __ A. make the lessons fun.
    __ B. punish the dog when it doesn't obey.
    __ C. take the dog to the veterinarian for training.
    __ D. don't feed the dog if it doesn't listen.

3. What is a grooming glove used for?

    __ A. It prevents you from getting hair on your hands when you groom your dog.
    __ B. You put them on your dog's paws when you give it a bath.
    __ C. It removes loose hair and dirt from a short-haired dog.
    __ D. It is used to clean the ears and tail of dogs with long hair.

4. Compared to a puppy, an older dog

    __ A. does not need as much water.
    __ B. cannot be trained.
    __ C. does not need to be rewarded.
    __ D. does not need to be fed as often.

5. What should you do if your dog is being disobedient?

    __ A. you give it a hug
    __ B. you give it a treat
    __ C. you praise him
    __ D. you say "no!" and stop playing with him for a while.

6. Puppies behave differently from grownup dogs. List two examples.

A puppy _____ A grown dog _____

_____ _____

A puppy _____ A grown dog _____

_____ _____

7. If your friend gives you one of the puppies from his or her dog's litter, what items will you need to buy to properly care for that dog? Why do you need these items?

_____

_____

_____

_____

_____

_____

_____

_____

_____

_____

_____

_____

_____

_____

_____

_____

_____

_____

_____

_____

_____

_____

_____

Exercise 5

Learning About Canoes

Canoes are long, narrow boats. The front and back of a canoe look almost exactly the same. This is why a canoe is called a double-ended boat. Because of its shape, a canoe is able to speed easily through the water.

Canoes were very important in the exploration and early history of North America. The North American Indians built and used canoes covered with animal hides and birch bark. The canoes that we use today are very similar to the Indian and explorer boats of long ago.

Canoes have many uses. They can be paddled on lakes, rivers, and the ocean. Many people like to take their canoes on long camping trips into the wilderness. A canoe can carry a heavy load of camping gear, food, and other supplies.

Modern canoes are much stronger and lighter than the old Indian skin-and-wood boats. Many different canoe models and styles are available today. Canoes are made from wood, fiberglass, metal, or plastic. Most modern canoes are durable and easy to repair.

A canoe that is used for recreational use is made of aluminum and is about 15 feet long. Boats like this are easy to handle by young paddlers on lakes and rivers.

The front end of a canoe is called the bow. The other end is called the stern. The top edges of the boat's sides are called the gunwales. Some canoes have a keel. A keel is a raised strip in the center of the canoe's bottom surface. A keel helps a canoe move forward through the water in a straight line. The horizontal bars bridging between the gunwales of a canoe are called thwarts. They give the boat added strength and can be leaned against while paddling.

Canoe paddles are made from many different materials including wood, plastic, and fiberglass, or aluminum. The flat part of the paddle is called the blade. The blade is the part that moves through the water. It is connected to a long, thin section called the shaft. The blade and shaft are joined at the throat.

The grip is the part that you hold onto while paddling. It is located on the shaft at the opposite end from the blade. Grips can be rounded, pear shaped, or have a T-grip to give good paddling control.

Safety is very important in canoeing. You must be a good swimmer before you can canoe. Always wear a life jacket when you canoe. They are called personal flotation devices or PFD. The life jackets will keep you afloat if your boat tips over or if you fall out of the canoe. The first thing you need to learn is how to get into a canoe and launch it safely. Empty canoes seem stable, but it is very easy to tip them over if you are not careful getting into them. You must keep your weight balanced near the center of the boat or the canoe will roll over and throw you into the water.

Entering a canoe from a small pier is easy when done correctly. The bow paddler gets in first, and the stern paddler is the last to go aboard. In the canoe you can either paddle sitting down or kneeling in the canoe. Kneeling keeps the boat's center of gravity, much lower than if you sit on the seat. Some paddlers kneel on one knee.

The basic paddling technique is called the forward stroke, which is also called the power or bow stroke. It is a very natural motion and is easy to learn. The back stroke is almost the exact opposite of the forward stroke. This stroke is used to slow down or back up a canoe. Other basic strokes are the draw stroke and the push stroke. These strokes will move the boat sideways.

When you are returning from your canoe trip, remember to pull the canoe well up on shore or tie it to a pier so it won't float away.

1. Where is the keel located on a canoe?

    __ A.   at the back end of the canoe
    __ B.   at the bottom surface of the canoe
    __ C.   between the gunwales
    __ D.   at the center of gravity

2. Why, do you think, the canoes were important to the explorers?

    __ A.   Canoes could be paddled on lakes, rivers, and the ocean.
    __ B.   Canoes were easy to carry over land.
    __ C.   It was easy to learn how to paddle a canoe.
    __ D.   Canoes didn't make a noise when sneaking up on people.

3. What material would a canoe builder NOT use to make a canoe?

    __ A.   aluminum
    __ B.   cloth
    __ C.   wood
    __ D.   plastic

4. Why must you wear a life jacket when you go on a canoeing trip?

    __ A.   to give good paddling control
    __ B.   to keep from falling out of the canoe
    __ C.   to keep you from drowning if you fall out of the canoe
    __ D.   to keep you warm

5. How do you keep from tipping over in a canoe?

    __ A.   You paddle fast to shore.
    __ B.   You stand up in the canoe.
    __ C.   You sit in the back of the canoe.
    __ D.   You kneel to keep the center of gravity low.

6. List two ways in which canoes and sail boats are similar:

_____

_____

_____

_____

_____

_____

_____

7. List two ways in which canoes and sail boats are different:

_____

_____

_____

_____

_____

8. Imagine that you are going on a canoe trip on Lake Hopatcong. How would you prepare yourself? What would you take with you?

_____

_____

_____

_____

_____

_____

_____

_____

_____

_____

_____

_____

_____

_____

_____

_____

_____

_____

_____

_____

_____

_____

_____

The ASK4 Language Arts Literacy test includes a writing assignment. You will be graded on your skills in language usage, grammar and the mechanics of writing. In this section of the workbook, you will review and practice some of those writing skills. Always refer to the Writer's Checklist on page 149 of this workbook before starting your writing project.

Using a Complete Sentence

Every sentence has two parts: the subject and the predicate. The subject is the person, place, or thing that the sentence is written about. The predicate, a single word or a group of words makes a statement about the subject. The most important element of the predicate is the **verb**.

The dog barked at the mailman.

In this sentence *dog* is the subject. The verb (or predicate) is *barked*.

Practice Exercise 1

Directions: In each sentence below, circle the subject and underline the verb.

1. [Raymond] drove his new car down the street.

2. England is a country rich in history.

3. The lightning struck a telephone pole.

4. The steak sizzled on the grill.

5. I walked the dog around the block.

6. My mother works for a television station.

7. The baby cried all night long.

8. You are my best friend.

A sentence can have more than one subject and/or more than one predicate.

Practice Exercise 2

Directions: *In each sentence below, circle all subjects and underline all predicates.*

1. The New Jersey Devils beat the Anaheim Mighty Ducks and won the Stanley Cup playoffs.

2. Carrie, Briana, and Courtney graduated from high school and went to college.

3. Trenton, Newark, Paterson, and Camden are cities in New Jersey.

4. Every morning Cameron eats breakfast, makes his bed, and walks to school.

5. David does well in math, Bobby does well in science, and Michael does well in reading.

6. The *Titanic* struck an iceberg and sank.

Using Capital Letters

Proper nouns are the names of specific persons, places, or things. Proper nouns should begin with a capital letter. Common nouns are names that do not refer to a specific person, place, or thing. Common nouns do not need to be capitalized. Below is a list of some common and proper nouns.

Common Noun	Proper Noun
street	Pennsylvania Avenue
state	New Jersey
month	November
house	White House
language	Spanish
continent	Africa
day	Tuesday

Practice Exercise 3

Directions: Underline the proper nouns that should be capitalized in each sentence.

1. We visited <u>betsy</u> <u>ross's</u> house when we went to <u>philadelphia</u>, <u>pennsylvania</u>, in <u>july</u>.

2. You and i should go to new york on thursday to watch a baseball game at shea stadium.

3. I think charles dickens, who wrote *oliver twist*, was a great english writer.

4. We took the garden state parkway all the way down to cape may.

5. The mayflower sailed from england and landed in plymouth, massachusetts.

6. Both kyle and sara like to read books about the moon, the sun, and the planet mars.

7. The teacher taught his students about hercules and the gods and goddesses of greek mythology.

8. Many people have tried to climb mt. everest, the tallest mountain in the world.

Using Correct End Punctuation

There are three types of sentences: One that makes a statement (declarative), one that asks a question (interrogative), and one that shows strong feeling (exclamatory). Each one of these types of sentences uses a different form of end punctuation.

Sentence Type	Punctuation mark	Example
Declarative	period	Sean studied and passed the test.
Interrogative	question mark	Did you study for the test?
Exclamatory	exclamation point	What a hard test that was!

Practice Exercise 4

Directions: Insert the correct punctuation mark at the end of each sentence.

1. What is your favorite amusement park ride<u>?</u>

2. I like the roller coaster the best

3. What a wild ride the Medusa is

4. I don't know how to ski yet

5. When did you learn to play soccer

6. Don't you dare break your glasses

7. Do you want to go to college

8. I asked him how to get to his house

9. Do not go to the playground after school

10. Stop

Using Plural and Possessive Nouns Correctly

Plural nouns are ones that refer to more than one person, place, or thing. Most plural nouns end in *–s, -es, or –ies*. Possessive nouns are ones that show ownership. An apostrophe and *-s* are used to indicate possession. A plural noun can also be a possessive noun. To show the possessive form of a noun that all ready ends in *–s*, just place the apostrophe at the end. Here are some examples:

Singular	Plural	Possessive	Plural and Possessive
cat	cats	the cat's paw	the cats' tails
girl	girls	the girl's book	the girls' locker room
coach	coaches	the coach's seat	the coaches' salaries
actress	actresses	the actress' script	the actresses' dressing rooms
baby	babies	the baby's rattle	the babies' diapers

Not all plural nouns ends in –*s*. Here are a few examples:

Singular	Plural	Possessive	Plural and Possessive
child	children	the child's toy	the children's teacher
man	men	the man's watch	the men's department
deer	deer	the deer's foot	the deer's environment

Practice Exercise 5

Directions: For each sentence write the correct form of the noun in the blank. The singular form of the noun you are to use is shown in brackets.

1. I borrowed the [*teacher*] ___teacher's___ book because I left mine at home.

2. The [*player*] _____ removed their caps for the national anthem.

3. All the [*tree*] _____ leaves turned color in the autumn.

4. The babysitter took the two [*child*] _____ toys away when she put them to bed.

5. Both [*woman*] _____ take the bus to work.

6. Ramone stacked the [*box*] _____ in the corner of the room.

7. The [*student*] _____ backpacks had to be kept in their lockers.

8. The [*fly*] _____ buzzed around the food at the picnic.

Using the Correct Word

Many writers have trouble deciding which homophone to use. Homophones are words that sound the same but are spelled differently and have different meanings. The following are only a few examples of the many homophones in the English language.

Homophones:

to, too, and two   its and it's
their, there, and they're   principal and principle
through and threw   weigh and way

Practice Exercise 6

Directions: Circle the correct homophone that should be used in each sentence.

1. Hans ate only [two, to, too] of his chicken fingers because he was not [two, to, too] hungry.

2. The [principle, principal] handed out the diplomas at graduation.

3. I want to [wear, where] my new blouse to the party [wear, where] everyone can see it.

4. [Its, It's] a beautiful day to go to the beach and sit in the [sun, son].

5. Jason bought his [sale, sail] boat when it was on [sale, sail].

6. After three months at [see, sea] the sailor could finally [see, sea] land.

7. Gina [through, threw] the basketball [through, threw] the hoop.

8. Heather painted her bedroom walls a [pale, pail] shade of [blew, blue].

9. The field trip was canceled [do, dew, due] to the bad [weather, whether].

10. [Their, There, They're] going to spend the week at [their, there, they're] beach house.

Writing Paragraphs

When you write a whole story you break it up into paragraphs. Each paragraph has a single purpose or thought. You always start a new line and indent the first word of a new paragraph so the reader knows that a new paragraph starts.

The first paragraph is the introductory paragraph. The second (and third and fourth, if you are writing a long story) are called body paragraphs. Paragraphs can be long, or short with just one or two sentences in it. The first sentence in a paragraph is usually the topic or main sentence.

Each story or composition also has an ending paragraph that summarizes, or tells you the ending of the story. Your complete story or essay should have at least three paragraphs.

Getting Ready to Write

The first step in writing is to choose the topic you want to write about. The writing assignments on the NJ ASK will give you a prompt in the form of either a picture or a poem. The prompt will help you to choose a topic.

The next step is the prewriting stage. In this stage you can make a list of facts or ideas you want to include in your writing. You can draw a story map, make a list of characters, or make notes on any details you want to include in your story.

Now you are ready to write your first draft. As you write your draft, keep these four points in mind:

- Be sure each paragraph has a topic sentence.
- Be sure each sentence in the paragraph sticks to the topic.
- Be sure your paragraphs follow a logical order.
- Be sure all the paragraphs relate to the main idea of your story or essay.

After you have written your draft, the final step is to proofread and edit your writing. Check for spelling, punctuation, word usage, and grammar.

Practice Exercise 7

Directions: Read each paragraph. Write a simple topic sentence on the blank line before each paragraph.

1. *I like to read the newspaper every day.*

The first section contains world news and the big events like disasters, where many people got injured or died. The second section is often where you will find local news about your town, county, and state. A third section is usually devoted to sports. Sunday editions often include additional sections such as comics, real estate, travel, business, and classified ads.

2._____

The monster dinosaur moved slowly up the hill as the sun came up. The earth shook and all the animals ran quickly to hide in the forest. They were very quiet and stayed behind the bushes, but the monster seemed to be able to smell the little critters and kept moving closer and closer.

3._____

Finally, everything was loaded onto the moving van. I went outside to say good bye to the neighbors. I was going to miss them. But at the same time I looked forward to the new house where I was going to live. I was curious about the kids that lived on the block and the new school where I will be starting 5th grade in the fall.

4._____

Sometimes I think I'd like to be a doctor and help people stay well. Other times I think I'd enjoy being a teacher and working with children. Then there are times when I'm sure I want to work with computers or become a writer. Whatever I decide, I'm sure I'll need to get a good education first.

5._____

There were no stores where people could buy what they needed like we do today. They had to make everything themselves. They had to make their own candles, bake their own bread, weave their own fabric, and sew their own clothes. Most people had to grow their own fruits and vegetables and preserve their foods for the winter months. All this work left little time for leisure.

6._____

My father uses it to keep track of the family budget and to download pictures from his camera. My mother uses it to send e-mails and to shop at home. My brother uses it to do research for school and to type and print out his reports. My sister uses it to download music and instant message her friends. I use it mainly to play games.

7. _____

You must be sure to feed your pet every day. At least two or three times a day you should take it for a walk. You will need to take it to the veterinarian to get rabies shots and other shots that will keep it from getting sick. It is also a good idea to give your dog regular flea treatments. Most of all, your dog will need love and affection.

Practice Exercise 8

*Directions: Reach each topic sentence below. Choose the sentence that **does not** support the topic.*

1. We have good reason to honor Benjamin Franklin.

    ___ A. He was one of our country's greatest statesmen.
    ___ B. He was an inventor who gave us the Franklin stove and bifocal glasses.
    X_ C. Thomas Jefferson was both a statesman and inventor, too.
    ___ D. Franklin is also remembered for his early experiments with electricity.

2. I love to go to the circus.

    ___ A. The trapeze and high wire acts always thrill me.
    ___ B. Carnivals have exciting rides and games.
    ___ C. I enjoy seeing the lions, tigers, and elephants perform tricks.
    ___ D. The clowns make me laugh all the time.

3. Be sure to bring money when you go to a theme park.

    ___ A. There are a lot of rides to choose from.
    ___ B. You must buy a ticket to enter the park.
    ___ C. You will need to buy lunch while you are there.
    ___ D. You have to pay to park your car.

4. A library has more than just books.

    ___ A. Most let you borrow movies on VHS and DVD.
    ___ B. Many have music CD's and cassettes that you can borrow.
    ___ C. Some also have computer stations where you can get onto the Internet.
    ___ D. Some people buy their books from on-line bookstores.

5. Many American holidays honor famous people in history.

    __ A. In January, we celebrate Martin Luther King Day.
    __ B. In February, we celebrate the birth of both George Washington and Abraham Lincoln.
    __ C. In October, we honor Christopher Columbus.
    __ D. In November, we eat turkey on Thanksgiving Day.

6. I can always find something to do when it rains.

    __ A. I enjoy doing jigsaw puzzles.
    __ B. I can play basketball or go skateboarding with my friends.
    __ C. I can curl up on the couch and read a book.
    __ D. Sometimes I watch television or play video games.

7. My favorite food is pizza.

    __ A. Sometimes I order it with pepperoni and mushrooms.
    __ B. I like the kind with cheese baked inside the crust.
    __ C. You can buy spaghetti and meatballs if you don't want pizza.
    __ D. I have even had dessert pizza with apples and cinnamon on top.

8. Darrel comes from a large family.

    __ A. I come from a small family.
    __ B. He has seven brothers and sisters.
    __ C. He has nine aunts and uncles.
    __ D. He has sixteen cousins.

Practice Exercise 9

Directions: Read each groups of sentences and decide the most logical order of ideas. Number the sentences in the order in which you think they should appear.

1.   3   The bell rang and we went to our classrooms.
     1   The bus dropped us off in the school parking lot.
     4   The teacher took attendance.
     5   We opened our math books and began the lesson.
     2   We went to our lockers and hung up our coats.

2. _____ After I got the part, my mother helped me memorize my lines.
   _____ After the play, everyone applauded, and I was happy.
   _____ I auditioned for a part in the school play.
   _____ I was nervous performing in front of my family and friends on opening night.
   _____ I practiced my lines for hours before the play.

3. _____ The doctor gave him medicine for his throat.
   _____ His mother made an appointment with the doctor.
   _____ Carlos woke up in the morning with a sore throat.
   _____ The following morning, Carlos felt better.
   _____ The doctor examined his throat and took his temperature.

4. _____ At the airport, she went through customs and checked her bags.
   _____ Finally, she left Paris and flew home to New Jersey.
   _____ Then she boarded a plane to England.
   _____ Emma took a taxi to the airport.
   _____ After two weeks in London, she went to Paris.

5. _____ In the summer, the flowers blossomed.
   _____ We watered the seeds every day.
   _____ In early spring we planted the seeds in plastic containers in our kitchen window.
   _____ When the plants were 2 feet high, we dug them up and planted them outside.
   _____ We cut the flowers and put them in vases around our house.

6. _____ We went into the theater and sat in the front row.
   _____ The lights went out and the movie began.
   _____ We bought our tickets for the first show.
   _____ We waited in line for the box office to open.
   _____ We stopped at the snack bar and bought popcorn to eat during the movie.

Exercise 1 – Picture Prompt

<u>Directions</u>: Using the picture as a guide, write a story about what might be happening. You may take notes, create a web, or do other prewriting work in the planning space. Then, write your story on the lines provided. Before you begin writing, you should refer to the Writer's Checklist on page 149. Refer to it as often as you need. When you have finished your story, read what you have written. Use the checklist to make certain that your writing is the best it can be.

Planning Space

Setting

Main Character

Title

Conflict

Resolution

Write your story

Exercise 2 – Picture Prompt

<u>Directions</u>: Using the picture as a guide, write a story about what might be happening. You may take notes, create a web, or do other prewriting work in the planning space. Then, write your story on the lines provided. Before you begin writing, you should refer to the Writer's Checklist on page 149. Refer to it as often as you need. After you write your story, read what you have written. Use the checklist to make certain that your writing is the best it can be.

Planning Space

Write your story here

_____

_____

_____

_____

_____

_____

_____

_____

_____

_____

_____

_____

_____

_____

_____

_____

_____

_____

_____

_____

_____

_____

_____

Exercise 3 – Picture Prompt

Directions: Using the picture as a guide, write a story about what might be happening. You may take notes, create a web, or do other prewriting work in the planning space. Then, write your story on the lines provided. Before you begin writing, you should refer to the Writer's Checklist on page 149. Refer to it as often as you need. After you write your story, read what you have written. Use the checklist to make certain that your writing is the best it can be.

Planning Space

Write your story

Exercise 4 – Picture Prompt

Directions: Using the picture as a guide, write a story about what might be happening. You may take notes, create a web, or do other prewriting work in the planning space. Then, write your story on the lines provided. Before you begin writing, you should refer to the Writer's Checklist on page 149. Refer to it as often as you need. After you write your story, read what you have written. Use the checklist to make certain that your writing is the best it can be.

Planning and Prewriting Space

Write your essay

Exercise 5 – Picture Prompt

<u>Directions</u>: Using the picture as a guide, write a story about what might be happening. You may take notes, create a web, or do other prewriting work in the planning space. Then, write your story on the lines provided. Before you begin writing, you should refer to the Writer's Checklist on page 149. Refer to it as often as you need. After you write your story, read what you have written. Use the checklist to make certain that your writing is the best it can be.

Planning and Prewriting Space

Write your essay:

Exercise 6 – Poem Prompt

In this poem, read the author's words of warning.

> *If you should meet a crocodile,*
> *Don't take a stick and poke him;*
> *Ignore the welcome in his smile,*
> *Be careful not to stroke him.*
> *For as he sleeps upon the Nile,*
> *He thinner gets and thinner;*
> *And whenever you meet a crocodile*
> *He's ready for his dinner.*

Has there ever been a time when someone tried to warn you or give you advice? You may or may not have taken that advice. Write about what you did and how you felt or what you would have done and how you would have felt if this did happen. If this has not happened to you, write about what might happen if it had.

- Who was it that gave you advice or a warning?
- What advice or warning were you given?
- Why do you think the person gave you this advice or warning?
- Did you follow the advice?
- Explain why you did or did not take the advice.
- Do you think you made the right decision? Explain why or why not.

You may take notes, create a web, or do other prewriting work in the planning space. Then write your essay on the lines provided. Before you begin writing, you should refer to the Writer's Checklist on page 149. Reread it as often as you need. When you are finished with your writing project, read what you have written. Use the checklist to make certain that your writing is the best it can be.

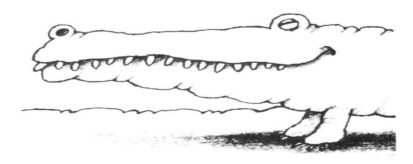

Planning Space

Write your essay here

Exercise 7 – Poem Prompt

In this poem, the author tells us to listen to the approaching rain. When you listen to this poem you can almost hear it too. Look up in the sky as the dark clouds come closer, listen to the sound of the wind, just before the first drops fall.

Whispers

rain
tells you its name
it whispers
round your house

in hushed tones
behind trees
through leaves
it whispers

I am near
I am near

before it is here
rain whispers
round the corners
of your house.
by Monica Kulling

Using the poem as a springboard to your composition, imagine that it's a Saturday morning. The sky is covered with dark clouds, and the weather report says it's going to rain today. What will you do today or wish you could do on this rainy day that you would not do on a sunny day?

- What is the situation?
- What do you do or wish you could do?
- Explain how it happens.
- What people, animals, or things do you include in your composition?

You may take notes, create a web, or do other prewriting work in the planning space. Then write your story on the lines provided. Refer to the Writer's Checklist on page 149.

Planning and Prewriting Space

Write your essay here

Writing Project: Picture Prompt

<u>Directions</u>: Using the picture as a guide, write a story about what might be happening. You may take notes, create a web, or do other prewriting work in the planning space. Then, write your story on the lines provided.

Before you begin writing, you should refer to the Writer's Checklist on page 149. Refer to it as often as you need. After you have written your story, go over the items and use the checklist to make certain that your writing is the best it can be.

Planning and Prewriting Space

Write your story here:

_____

_____

_____

_____

_____

_____

_____

_____

_____

_____

_____

_____

_____

_____

_____

_____

_____

Reading: Narrative

Directions: Read the following text carefully. Then answer the multiple choice and open-ended questions that follow. Select the correct or best answer from the four choices given. The open-ended questions will sometimes ask to draw a conclusion based on the story or to summarize the story you have read. Make sure you answer all parts of these questions.

Robinson Crusoe on the Island
adapted from the story by Daniel Defoe

The storm started in the morning and kept getting worse. All day and all night our ship rocked from one side and then to the other. On the evening of the second day a huge wave, as big as a mountain, came rolling toward our already severely damaged ship. It broke over us with a crash, and down came our sails.

We saw land in the distance, but the shore looked rocky. The wild winds had driven our ship so far off course that we had no idea what land we were near.

I was hanging onto the railing when the ship hit a rock. In that wild water we could not hope to have the ship hold together much longer without breaking into pieces. The men called from below that she was already taking in water.

At once, we put down a little boat over the ship's side and, all getting into it, we braved the wild sea.

The wind drove us toward the land, but it did not look inviting. A giant wave rolled over us. It upset the boat, throwing us into the water. We were all swallowed up that second.

Nothing can tell how I felt when I sank in the water. Though I swam well, I could not get above water to draw a breath. That wave drove me and carried me a good way toward the land, and, having spent itself, it rolled back and left me able to touch the bottom.

I tried to get to my feet and walk forward before another wave would return and take me up again. But I could not move fast enough. I saw the sea come after me as high as a great hill and as angry as an old enemy. So I tried to hold my breath and raise myself upon the water, if I could.

The wave that came upon me buried me at once twenty or thirty feet deep in its own body. I could feel myself carried a great distance. I held my breath and tried to swim forward with all my strength.

I was ready to burst with holding my breath when I felt myself finally coming up. My head shot out above the water. Though I could keep myself up for only two or three seconds, those seconds gave me

9

the air I needed. When the water began to <u>recede</u>, I felt ground again with my feet. Then I ran with what strength I had left onto the island. There I climbed quickly up on a little hill where I was out of reach of the water.

When I caught my breath, I walked about, calling out for my friends, but there did not seem to be one person saved but me. The sea buried all the rest.

Night was coming upon me. I didn't know if there were wild animals nearby. My only hope, I thought, was to climb high into a tree.

11 There I would find a place so I could sleep without falling to earth. I found a large bushy tree nearby and I climbed. Feeling more tired than ever before in my life, I fell asleep, though it rained and stormed all night.

In the morning I saw to my surprise that my ship, which had been caught on the rocks, was not broken to pieces. She lay, as the wind and sea had tossed her, upon the land about two miles on my right.

I walked as far as I could toward her. But I found on a wide neck of water between me and the ship, so I pulled off my shirt and started swimming.

When I came to the ship I wondered how to get on board. As she

14 lay <u>grounded</u> and high out of the water, there was nothing within my reach to lay hold of. I swam around her and spotted a small piece of rope hanging over the side. With much trouble I got hold of it, and with the help of that rope I climbed up and got on board.

First I went to the bread room. The food was dry. Being very hungry, I filled my pockets with bread. I ate it as I went about other things, for I had no time to lose. From the wood on board, I needed to build a raft.

It was a small raft, so I had to think carefully of what was most important to take back with me right away. I decided on a box of bread, rice, cheeses and dried meat.

While I was doing this, the tide began to wash out to sea. As I looked back across the neck of water, I saw my shirt, which I had left on the sand, swim away.

This set me hunting for clothes, of which I found enough, but I took no more than I needed.

I had other things in mind, for which I had greater need. First, tools for building. I found a box of tools which was indeed a prize to me, better than gold at the time.

For most of the next four weeks I went back and forth to the ship again and again, bringing all I could to my island. But then the calm tropical weather turned stormy again and it became most difficult to reach the ship.

The storm blew very hard for several days and nights, and then it suddenly calmed down. In the morning when I looked out, there was no more ship to be seen.

I felt glad that I had gotten everything out of the ship that I could use. When I had used up all the food I had salvaged from the ship I went out to search for berries and hunt for small animals. I made a fishing pole and fastened a string with a hook at the end. The fish were plentiful around the island. For cooking I made a pot of clay which I baked in the hot sun. I made a tent out of leftover sail from the ship to keep me dry during the frequent tropical storms. I found some caves nearby and often spent the night in one of them to keep out of the wind and rain.

One day, as I was busy inside my cave, I was terribly frightened with a most surprising thing indeed, for all of a sudden, the ground I stood on shook.

A great piece of rock fell near me with a loud noise and the top of my cave was falling in. I was afraid to be buried in it, so I ran outside. I had no sooner stepped out that I knew my island was in the middle of a terrible earthquake. The sea came alive with waves higher than buildings. The earth-quake must have been even stronger under the water than on the island. I had never experienced an earthquake before and was sick with fear. I could think of nothing but the hill falling on my tent and burying all my goods. I sat up all night afraid of falling asleep not knowing what to do. The downpour of rain kept me wet and cold. The wind rose higher and roared through the trees as if it were trying to tear them up by their roots.

I was close to being blown away in the storm that followed the earthquake so I had to go back into my cave. But I was very much afraid it would fall on my head.

The fear of being swallowed alive would not let me sleep, but by morning my eyes were so heavy that I dropped off for a few hours. As soon as I woke up I decided that if the island had earthquakes, there would be no living for me in a cave. I must build a little place for myself in an open space, or I was certain at one time or another to be buried alive.

1. Why does the ship's crew leave the ship and get into the small boat?

    ___ A. because it was easier to get to shore
    ___ B. because they thought the ship was about to sink
    ___ C. because the shore looked rocky
    ___ D. because the crew wanted to explore the land

2. In paragraph 9 the author writes, "When the water began to recede, I felt ground again with my feet." What does the word recede mean in this sentence?

    ___ A. get colder
    ___ B. grow calmer
    ___ C. move away
    ___ D. get deeper

3. What happened to the other men from the ship?

    ___ A. They sailed home in the lifeboat.
    ___ B. They swam to the island.
    ___ C. They drowned.
    ___ D. They were rescued by another ship.

4. Where did Robinson Crusoe spend his first night on the island?

    ___ A. on the rocks
    ___ B. on the raft
    ___ C. on the beach
    ___ D. in a tree

5. In paragraph 14 the author writes that the ship was "…grounded and high out of the water." What does the word grounded mean in this sentence?

    ___ A. stuck on the ground
    ___ B. punished
    ___ C. destroyed by a wave
    ___ D. sunken

6. Robinson Crusoe builds a small wooden raft to

    __ A. try to sail back home.
    __ B. take his supplies from the ship to the island.
    __ C. get from the island back to his ship.
    __ D. try to rescue his fellow crewmen.

7. Which of the following things doesn't Robinson Crusoe bring to the island from the ship?

    __ A. clothing
    __ B. gold
    __ C. tools
    __ D. food

8. What word best describes Robinson Crusoe in this story?

    __ A. lonely
    __ B. frightened
    __ C. resourceful
    __ D. helpless

9. What would be another good title for this story?

    __ A. Stranded
    __ B. Adventures at Sea
    __ C. The Life of Robinson Crusoe
    __ D. The Big Wave

10. If you were on a deserted island, what items do you think would be most useful to have in order to survive?

_____

_____

_____

_____

_____

_____

_____

_____

_____

_____

_____

_____

_____

_____

_____

_____

_____

_____

_____

_____

_____

_____

11. In paragraph 11 the author writes that Crusoe "didn't know if there were wild animals nearby." Give one example of why it would be good to have animals on the island. Give one example of why it might be bad.

_____

_____

_____

_____

_____

_____

_____

_____

_____

_____

_____

_____

_____

_____

_____

_____

_____

_____

_____

_____

_____

12. The author of this story describes how Robinson Crusoe reacts to a dangerous situation. Imagine you were in a similar position. In what ways would you react the same as Robinson Crusoe did? In what ways would you react differently? Organize your thoughts by filling in the comparison chart below.

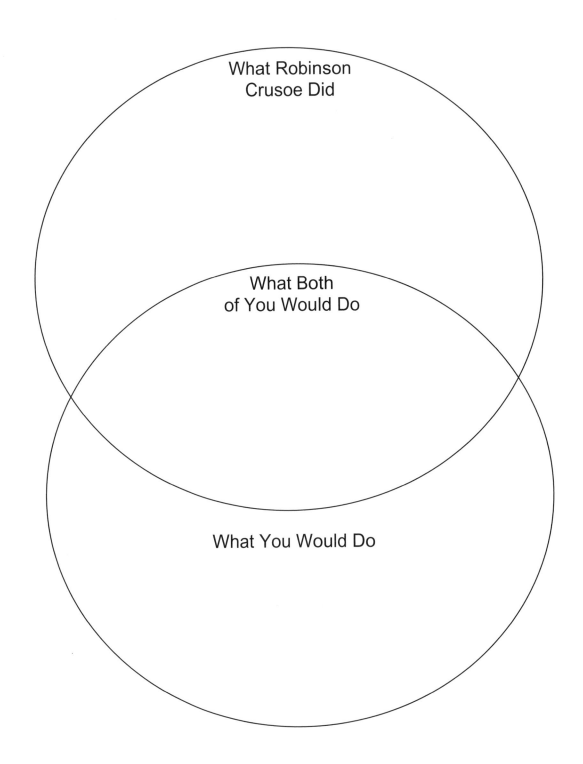

What Robinson
Crusoe Did

What Both
of You Would Do

What You Would Do

From Knights in Days of Old
by Ellen Javernick

Modern-day baseball players practice by hitting balls thrown to them by pitching machines. Basketball players use machines to get the balls back to them. Medieval athletes had their own mechanical practice devices. When young nobles and princes practiced spearing metal rings, to prepare for their tournaments, they rode wooden horses on a rotating platform.

The practicing knights are long, long gone. But through the centuries the rotating horses have stayed with us. And we are now the ones who go merrily around on this merry-go-round, or carousel. "Carousel"—the word tells the story. It comes from the name those first riders called their tournaments.

3 More than a hundred years ago, carousels came to the United States. Wood-carvers created them during the long winter months, and in summer the carousels traveled to the fairs. Each horse was unique. As the century wore on, some were carved to look like Kentucky Derby winners, their heads circled with wooden flowers. Some were carved to look like cowboy ponies. Others resembled the splendid <u>steeds</u> of the knights of medieval times.

Early carousels were built as simple horse-powered machines. When portable steam engines were invented, carousels became more popular and practical. But it wasn't until the 1880s that carousels really got going.

At that time electricity was new and exciting, even a little scary. So people hesitated to ride on the new, electrically powered trolley cars. To attract riders, the trolley companies routed their lines to public beaches, where marvelous carousels were constructed. Eager children persuaded their parents to let them ride the wooden horses.

Families frequently spent the whole day there, returning home in the evening after a last electrically powered carousel ride. Tired children strained their ears to hear the organ music floating from the carousel they had left behind. They tried to catch a final glimpse of the hundred twinkling lights reflecting from the decorative mirrors.

7 Making carousels became big business. There was a sudden demand for carvers of the animal figures and decorations. Many furniture makers turned into carousel carvers. <u>Apprentice</u> carvers rounded out the bodies. More practiced carvers were in charge of the legs and saddles. Master craftsmen carved the heads. The inward sides of the animals were as carefully carved as the outward sides, but not as elaborately, since they did not show. And when carousels had several rows of animals, those on the inside rows were not as elaborately carved as those on the outside. But the heads were always very fine.

For variety, some carvers also made lions, giraffes, and even elephants. Nor did they stop with animals to ride. They carved seats for parents with babies and others who preferred to sit. A carousel in Denver has a seat like a chariot, decorated with historical figures and the Statue of Liberty. The tops of carousels were decorated also with carvings of everything from rosy-cheeked angels to fierce dragons.

Brass poles ran from the floor of the carousel up to the canopy. On these the beautiful animals rode up and down. Around the outside of the carousel, rings were suspended, all of steel except for one of brass. Riders on the outer row could lean out and try to catch a ring as they went by. "Spearing" the brass ring earned a free ride.

10 Soon thousands of carousels twirled all over the United States. They were also called whirligigs, flying jennies, and carry-us-alls. Perhaps they would all still be there if the Depression had not put an end to the amusement parks in the 1930s. During the Depression many people lost their jobs; nobody had money to spend on carousels. Most of the amusement parks were closed, the lights turned off, the organs silenced. The wooden horses sat empty, easy prey for the wind and rain.

11 A few were revived after World War II, but today those few are dwindling. In 1989, according to the National Carousel Associates, fewer than 150 operating wooden carousels remained in this country, down from the 322 of 1979. One reason for their disappearance is their increasing value as collectors' items. In 1989 one horse sold for $101,750, and a rooster for $148,500.

Fortunately, groups like the National Carousel Association are working hard to save the remaining wooden carousels by having them designated as historical landmarks. Every year its members gather for four days of fun-filled events that allow members to admire and ride as many different carousels as possible. The organization also raises funds to repair the carousels and restore them to their original finely crafted splendor and preserve this unique art form.

Few carousels now have the brass ring game, because riders might fall off and hurt themselves. So there is scarcely a free ride to be won, let alone victory in a tournament. But the circling animals still bring a reward, as they always have. The prize today is a journey back in time.

1. In paragraph 3 the author writes, "Others resembled the splendid <u>steeds</u> of the knights of old." What does the word <u>steeds</u> mean in this sentence?

   __ A. spears
   __ B. suits of armor
   __ C. tournaments
   __ D. horses

2. Carousels became very popular in the United States when what modern development took place?

   __ A. electricity
   __ B. the automobile
   __ C. organ music
   __ D. amusement parks

3. In paragraph 7 the author writes, "<u>Apprentice</u> carvers rounded out the bodies." Based on context clues, what type of person is an <u>apprentice</u>?

   __ A. one who is familiar with horses
   __ B. one who is learning a craft
   __ C. one who does poor quality work
   __ D. one who works with wood

4. Which of the following is not another name for the carousel?

    __ A. merry-go-round
    __ B. carry-us-all
    __ C. Ferris wheel
    __ D. whirligig

5. What did the early American carousels have in common with those of Medieval days?

    __ A. They both had a variety of animals from which a rider could choose.
    __ B. They both played music.
    __ C. Riders on both could try to catch a brass ring.
    __ D. On both carousels, the more beautifully carved horses were placed on the outside.

6. What event caused the carousel to lose its popularity?

    __ A. the start of World War II
    __ B. the invention of the roller coaster
    __ C. a shortage of wood
    __ D. the Depression years when many people lost their jobs

7. In paragraph 10 the author writes, "The wooden horses sat empty, easy prey for the wind and rain." What does the author mean by this sentence?

    __ A. Left unprotected in the rain and wind, the carousel horses eventually rotted and fell apart.
    __ B. Bad weather kept people from riding the carousels.
    __ C. The wind and rain kept the carousel horses clean and looking like new.
    __ D. The carousels ran on electricity and had to be turned off whenever it rained.

8. In paragraph 11 the author writes, "A few were revived after World War II, but today those few are <u>dwindling</u>." What is the best synonym for <u>dwindling</u>?

    ___ A. growing
    ___ B. improving
    ___ C. decreasing
    ___ D. continuing

9. According to the article, one of the goals of the National Carousel Association is to

    ___ A. open more amusement parks with carousels.
    ___ B. get the government to recognize that carousels are collectors' items.
    ___ C. improve safety conditions on amusement park rides.
    ___ D. provide money to preserve carousels

10. What is the most likely reason that carousel makers placed colored lights and mirrors on top of the rides?

    ___ A. so that owners could keep the ride open at night
    ___ B. so that the ride would look much larger than it actually was
    ___ C. so that airplanes could see them at night
    ___ D. so that the rides would be safe for children

11. What is the author's main purpose in writing this article?

    ___ A. to persuade people to become woodcarvers
    ___ B. to tell the history of the carousel
    ___ C. to persuade people to join the National Carousel Association
    ___ D. to interest people in buying a used carousel horse

12. The carousel goes round and round in a circle and up and down. What other fun things go round and round or up and down?

_____

_____

_____

_____

_____

_____

_____

_____

_____

_____

_____

_____

_____

_____

_____

_____

_____

_____

_____

_____

_____

_____

_____

13. Imagine that you have a friend or relative who has never seen a carousel. Write a letter to him or her and describe a carousel.

_____

_____

_____

_____

_____

_____

_____

_____

_____

_____

_____

_____

_____

_____

_____

_____

_____

_____

_____

_____

_____

_____

_____

_____

Writing: Poem Prompt

Directions: Read the following poem to yourself while it is read to you, then you will complete a writing task.

In this poem, the author remembers the past and reminds us that, by living right every day, we will always have fond memories and we can hope for happiness in the future.

> *"For Yesterday is but a Dream,*
> *and Tomorrow is only a Vision,*
> *But Today,*
> *Well lived, makes every Yesterday*
> *A Dream of Happiness*
> *And every Tomorrow a Vision of Hope."*

Has there ever been a time when you have made somebody happy by doing or saying something nice, that has given that person a happy memory of the event. Or, write about a time when somebody did something nice for you that gives you happy memories.

- What was the situation?
- What did you do or say to make that person feel better?
- If you did accomplish this, explain how it happened.
- Was that person a stranger, friend, or a member of your family?
- If you tried to make that person happy, but did not succeed, explain why.
- Explain how you might be successful in accomplishing this in the future.

You may take notes, create a web, or do other prewriting work in the planning space. Then write your essay on the lines provided. Before you begin writing, you should refer to the Writer's Checklist on page 149. Reread it as often as you need. After you write your essay, read what you have written. Use the checklist to make certain that your writing is the best it can be.

Planning and Pre-writing space:

_____

_____

_____

_____

_____

_____

_____

_____

_____

_____

_____

_____

_____

_____

_____

_____

_____

_____

_____

_____

_____

_____

_____

_____

Write your essay here:

_____

_____

_____

_____

_____

_____

_____

_____

_____

_____

_____

_____

_____

_____

_____

_____

_____

_____

_____

_____

_____

_____

_____

_____

_____

_____

_____

Writing Project A: Picture Prompt

Directions: Using the picture as a guide, write a story about what might be happening. You may take notes, create a web, or do other prewriting work in the planning space. Then, write your story on the lines provided. Before you begin writing, you should refer to the Writer's Checklist on page 149. Refer to it as often as you need. After you write your story, read what you have written. Use the checklist to make certain that your writing is the best it can be.

Planning and prewriting space:

_____

_____

_____

_____

_____

_____

_____

_____

_____

_____

_____

_____

_____

_____

_____

_____

_____

_____

_____

_____

_____

_____

_____

_____

_____

Write your essay here:

Reading: Narrative

Directions: Read the following story. Then answer the multiple-choice and open-ended questions that follow.

Betty sat peeling apples. She wasn't peeling them to eat. She was trying to cut an all-in-one-piece apple peel. When she did, she tossed the peel over her shoulder, calling: "Apple tree! Show my true love's name to me!" Betty turned round and saw the peel shaped like a letter J. She would marry a man whose name began with J.

She considered the J's she knew. "Jack is too old. John is already engaged. Jim is only nine years old. Jan! He's not too old or too young. And he's not dating anybody."

Betty decided that Jan would be her man, and in no time at all they were married, for Betty nearly always got what she wanted.

Each day Jan went to work, leaving Betty at home with his mother, who thought up chores for Betty to do all day. Betty didn't like to work. She cried, knowing it upset Jan to see her so unhappy.

"What will please you?" he asked. "Tell me and I'll do it."

"Having my own house will make me happy," Betty said.

By the year's end Jan had built her a house. When she saw it, Betty clapped her hands with delight. They moved into the new house and Betty was happy for a while. Each morning Jan went to work, and Betty stayed in bed, sometimes until afternoon. But Jan did not complain, for if Betty was happy, then so was he.

Soon there were cobwebs hanging from the ceiling and dust balls in the corners. The windows were so dirty that the sun was shut out. Betty was unhappy again. "You see other people when you go to work, but I must sit here alone. I need company."

The next evening Jan came home with a small kitten. Betty was not lonely anymore; she had Tabby for company. Jan did not mind that the house was dirty or that his supper was burnt, for if Betty was happy, then so was he.

But the evening came when Jan got home to find the cat howling in one corner and Betty howling in another. "Tabby has no one to play with, and I have no one to talk to."

"What is it you want?" Jan asked.

"A baby."

The following winter, there was a baby in the house. For a while everything went well. Betty loved the baby and was happy. But the baby sometimes fretted and fussed and was a bit of a bother. So Betty would leave him in the house alone and go to town to shop and so she would not have to listen to the crying. "He'll be all right," she said. "It's just for a short time, and he has Tabby for company."

One afternoon Betty lingered in town longer than usual. It was already dusk when she started back home. She hurried as fast as she could, for she didn't want Jan to get back before she did. When she got home, the door was open. But no smoke curled from the chimney, and no light shone from the windows. When Betty looked inside, there was no one there!

She cried so hard that Jan heard her as he walked home. The neighbors heard her and came running to see what was wrong.

"My baby is gone!" she sobbed.

Jan, filled with rage and grief, shouted. "Find the baby, or you'll lose your husband, too."

Betty ran out into the moonlit night to look for the baby. Jan and the neighbors went out, too. There was no sign of the child. At daybreak, the neighbors went home, and Jan returned to the house.

As the sun rose, Betty heard a sound coming from beneath a bush. She parted the branches and saw Tabby sitting next to the baby who was fast asleep beneath the bush.

Betty picked up her baby and ran to the house, with Tabby close behind. When Jan saw his son, he cried with joy. The neighbors heard him and came to see if the baby was safe.

One woman spied a dirty mark, no bigger than a freckle, on the baby's foot. "The fairies took that child," she said. "They tried to wash him from head to toe, but the sun scared them off. Mark my words. They will try to take him again unless you're careful!" the woman said.

Betty was careful not to let the baby out of her sight. She kept everything clean all the time, too, but no matter how hard she scrubbed, she could not wash away the dirty spot from the baby's foot.

"A fairy mark," her neighbor called it.

"A lucky spot" Betty said. For it would remind her that she had everything she needed to make her happy. Jan was happy too.

1. What would Betty have done if the all-in-one-piece apple peel had landed in the shape of an M?

    ___ A. She would peel another apple to get married some day.
    ___ B. She would have a child whose name began with an M.
    ___ C. She would marry someone whose name began with an M.
    ___ D. She would marry in a month beginning with the letter M.

2. Why did Betty want to move to her own house?

    ___ A. Because she didn't want her mother-in-law telling her what to do all day.
    ___ B. She wanted a cat and her mother-in-law wouldn't let her have one.
    ___ C. There was not enough room in her mother-in-law's house for three adults, a cat and a baby.
    ___ D. Her mother-in-law had a dirty house.

3. What does Jan mean when he tells Betty "you'll lose your husband, too"?

    ___ A. The windows in the cottage are so dirty that she won't be able to see him.
    ___ B. If she doesn't find the baby, he will leave her.
    ___ C. When he goes off into the night to look for the baby, he might not find his way back.
    ___ D. He wants to go back to live with his mother because Betty is a terrible cook and housekeeper.

4. Why did Betty want a baby?

    __ A. She wanted to please her husband.
    __ B. She didn't want the cat any more.
    __ C. It was too quiet in the house.
    __ D. She thought the baby would make her happy.

5. What words would best describe Betty before she lost her child?

    __ A. happy and carefree
    __ B. careful and thoughtful
    __ C. angry and careless
    __ D. lazy and selfish

6. What kind of a person do you think Betty became after the events in this story?

    __ A. a lazy person
    __ B. a good mother
    __ C. a gentle person
    __ D. a liar

7. What best describes Jan in this story?

    __ A. He is lazy.
    __ B. He has a bad temper.
    __ C. He likes to make Betty happy.
    __ D. He likes to play with his son.

8. What would be a good title for this story?

    __ A. Betty's Baby
    __ B. Tabby Saves the Day
    __ C. The All-in-one piece Apple Peel
    __ D. Betty is Happy at Last

9. The conflict is the main problem in a story.

   - What is the conflict in this story?
   - How is it resolved?

   _____

   _____

   _____

   _____

   _____

   _____

   _____

   _____

   _____

   _____

   _____

   _____

   _____

   _____

   _____

   _____

   _____

   _____

   _____

   _____

   _____

   _____

   _____

10. When Betty's baby is found and brought home, a neighbor sees a small mark on the baby's foot.

   Why does the neighbor call the mark a "fairy mark"?
   Why does Betty call it a "lucky spot"?

   _____

   _____

   _____

   _____

   _____

   _____

   _____

   _____

   _____

   _____

   _____

   _____

   _____

   _____

   _____

   _____

   _____

   _____

   _____

   _____

   _____

   _____

Writing Project B - Poem Prompt

Directions: Read the following poem to yourself while it is read to you. Then complete the writing task. Ideas from the poem may help you with your writing.

Writing: Poem Prompt

The inner side of every cloud
is bright and shining.
I therefore turn my clouds about
And always wear them inside out
To show the lining.

When the author talks about the clouds in this poem he really means something that makes us sad, like something bad or sad happening to you or a family member. When you feel sad about something, then you should think of something that will make you feel better. That's like turning a cloud inside out to cheer you up.

Using the poem as a springboard to your own essay, write about a time when you were told something that made you sad but then you thought of something that cheered you up, or somebody helped you so you didn't feel sad any more.

Refer to the Writer's Checklist on page 149 to make sure your writing is the best you can.

Planning and Prewriting Space

Write your essay here:

_____

_____

_____

_____

_____

_____

_____

_____

_____

_____

_____

_____

_____

_____

_____

_____

_____

_____

_____

_____

_____

_____

_____

_____

_____

<u>**Introduction:**</u> Kelly is a 6th grader who has recently completed a first aid course. One Saturday afternoon during the summer Kelly was babysitting her cousins Todd and Ryan. Todd and Ryan were playing in the backyard when suddenly Kelly heard Ryan crying. When Kelly got to the backyard, Todd told Kelly that Ryan had been stung by a bee. Kelly noticed that Ryan was also having trouble breathing and had a small cut on his knee. Kelly was relieved that she remembered what she was taught at the first aid course and had a copy of the pamphlet Emergency Basics.

The pamphlet is printed here to you can decide how Kelly should handle Ryan's injuries. As you read the pamphlet, feel free to write in the text or underline important information. After you have finished reading "Emergency Basics," answer the multiple-choice and open-ended questions that follow:

EMERGENCY BASICS

Use this information until a health care professional can be reached:

Emergency first aid for a baby or child who..

has a <u>HEAD INJURY</u> from a fall or a blow to the head:

Warning signs:

- Any loss of consciousness after an injury
- Inability to move arms or legs
- Blood coming out of nose, mouth, or ears
- Has a headache, is dizzy, or won't stop vomiting
- Pupils of the eyes are uneven in size
- Cannot be awakened

What to do:

Try to have the child rest quietly and call the doctor or 911 <u>immediately</u>.

has been SCALDED OR BURNED:

What to do:

- If the injury is to an arm or leg, place it in cool water; if the injury is to another part of the body, immediately apply a clean cloth dipped in cool water.
- Call the doctor or 911.
- Leave any blisters alone.
- Keep the area free of ointments, greases, or powders.
- Cover the area loosely with a clean material that won't stick to the wounds – such as aluminum foil – until help arrives.

is CUT AND BLEEDING:

What to do:

- If the child is bleeding from a cut, place a clean bandage over the cut and apply direct pressure for several minutes.
- When bleeding stops, wash the cut gently with warm water.
- Apply a nonstick dressing or bandage.

Call doctor if:

- Bleeding does not stop.
- Edges of the wound are widely separated.
- Cut is from a human or animal bite.
- If the area becomes red or if there is discharge.

may have been POISONED:

What to do:

- Determine what the child has swallowed and the quantity, if possible.
- Immediately call 911.

has a BEE STING OR INSECT BITE:

Some allergic reactions may require <u>immediate</u> medical attention. These include hives, chest tightness, sudden hoarseness, wheezing or noisy, difficulty breathing, difficulty swallowing, swelling in the face, dizziness, cold clammy skin, or total collapse. Call 911 to get immediate emergency attention.

Bee Sting:

- Most stings are not serious and result only in temporary pain and swelling at the sting site.

What to do:

- If the stinger remains in the skin, gently remove it with a sideways scraping motion or remove it at the skin surface with tweezers.

Insect Bites:

Most insect bites are not serious. You will see a bit of swelling around the bite site that goes away in a day or so.

What to do:

- Most bites can be treated with cold compresses followed by calamine lotion or a paste of baking soda and water.
- Discourage the child from scratching. If itching is severe, a doctor can prescribe a medicine to help.
- If the bite becomes infected (redness and swelling around the bite), call a doctor or take the child to the Emergency room at a hospital immediately.

1. Based on Ryan's condition, Kelly should follow the instructions in what section of "Emergency Basics" first?

    ___ A. has a Head Injury
    ___ B. has been Scalded or Burned
    ___ C. may have been Poisoned
    ___ D. has a Bee Sting or Insect Bite

2, What is the **first** thing Kelly should do to help Ryan?

    ___ A. apply a cold compress on the sting.
    ___ B. immediately call 911
    ___ C. apply calamine lotion to the sting site
    ___ D. make Ryan stop crying.

3. Kelly looks in the pamphlet for information that could help her to assist Ryan. What information does she find **most** helpful?

    __ A. How to handle a crying child
    __ B. What to do about a bleeding cut
    __ C. The warning signs of an allergic reaction to a bee sting
    __ D. A list of doctors in the town

4. Kelly notices that the bee stinger is still in Ryan's leg. What should she do while waiting for the ambulance?

    __ A. Try to remove the stinger, then apply a cold compress, then calamine lotion
    __ B. Apply a hot compress and put a bandage on the sting
    __ C. Wash the area of the sting
    __ D. Elevate the leg and put ice on the sting

5. Kelly discovers there is no calamine lotion in the medicine chest to apply to the bee sting. What does the booklet say she can use instead?

    __ A. liquid soap
    __ B. baking soda mixed with water
    __ C. rubbing alcohol
    __ D. paper towel

6. If Ryan only cut his leg, but was not stung by a bee, Kelly should call 911 if

    __ A. Ryan is crying.
    __ B. the bleeding does not stop.
    __ C. the bleeding stops right away and Ryan wants to play.
    __ D. Kelly can't find a bandage.

7. Do you think Kelly was smart? _____

How would you describe Kelly's handling of the situation?

_____

_____

8. Some medical emergencies are definitely more serious than others. Which medical emergency mentioned in the pamphlet seems most serious to you? Explain why you think it is very serious, using information from the pamphlet.

_____

_____

_____

_____

_____

_____

_____

_____

_____

_____

_____

_____

_____

_____

Vocabulary

audience	the person or people who read an author's story.
author	the person who writes the story.
autobiography	a true story of a person's life written by that person.
biography	a story written about the life of an actual person.
central idea	the main idea or point of a story.
character trait	a quality or characteristic of one of a story's characters.
climax	the point of greatest suspense in a story.
compare	to see how two or more people, places, or things are similar and how they are different.
conclusion	the conclusion is the end of the story.
conflict	the conflict is the main problem in the story.
context	the words or sentences next to or surrounding a specific word, phrase, or sentence.
contrast	to compare two or more people, places, or things, and to point out their differences.
definition	the meaning of a word.
dialogue	the conversation between characters in a story.
example	something chosen to show the nature or character of the rest; a sample.
fable	a fictional tale that teaches a moral lesson.
fact	a true statement that can be proved with evidence.

fairy tale	a made up story about fairies, giants, witches, and magic deeds.
fiction	a story that is made up or imagined.
folk tale	a story made up and handed down orally from one generation to the next generation.
hero	the main male character in a book.
heroine	the main female character in a book.
legend	a story about a hero or saint, handed down by tradition from earlier times.
main character	the most important character in a story.
main idea	the most important idea or point in a story.
main problem	the most important problem or conflict in a story.
mystery	a story about the unknown, the unexplained, or a secret.
narrator	the person in a story that tells what is happening.
nonfiction	a story or book that is based on actual events.
opinion	a belief or judgment not based on absolute certainty or fact.
paragraph	a group of sentences that tell one main idea.
plot	what happens in a story. A plot usually contains three parts: a problem, a climax, and a resolution.

resolution	the resolution of a story comes when the main problem is solved.
science fiction	an imaginative story involving actual or projected science.
sequence	the following of one thing after another, in a logical or time order.
setting	where and when a story takes place.
supporting detail	a sentence that presents information that supports the main idea the author is trying to make.
synonyms	words that have similar meanings.
villain	the character in a story who does bad or evil things.

When you are asked to write a story, refer to the following checklist:

Always remember to

[   ]   keep the central idea or topic in mind

[   ]   keep your audience in mind

[   ]   support your ideas with details, explanations, and examples

[   ]   state your ideas in a clear sequence

[   ]   include an opening and closing

[   ]   use a variety of words and vary your sentence structure

[   ]   state your opinion or conclusion clearly

[   ]   capitalize, spell, and use punctuation correctly

[   ]   write neatly